Designing and Drafting
for Handweavers

Designing and Drafting for Handweavers

BASIC PRINCIPLES
OF CLOTH CONSTRUCTION

Berta Frey

COLLIER BOOKS
A Division of Macmillan Publishing Co., Inc.
New York

COLLIER MACMILLAN PUBLISHERS
London

Macmillan Publishing Co., Inc.
866 Third Avenue, New York, N.Y. 10022
Collier Macmillan Canada, Inc.

Library of Congress Cataloging in Publication Data

Frey, Berta.
    Designing and drafting for handweavers.

    Includes index.
    1. Hand weaving. I. Title.
TT848.F7 1975   746.1'4   75-6739
ISBN 0-02-011400-1

10   9   8   7   6   5   4

Printed in the United States of America

Acknowledgments

To acknowledge all the help and encouragement I have had in the preparation of this book would be to list individually all my friends and to list in capitals all my weaver friends.

Where I have used drawings or samples from friends and students, I have given their names with their work. I sincerely hope there are no mistakes or omissions. If there are mistakes, certainly they are not intentional.

Especial thanks are due William P. Robinson of the Robinson Recording Laboratories in Philadelphia for all the time and effort he spent in making most of the photographs.

Most of all, I wish to thank Berta Harttmann, who helped so much. Without her generous assistance the book might still not be finished.

B. F.

Woodstock, New York

Contents

Introduction

Styles in fabrics change from year to year, but the basic principles of cloth construction remain constant. In handweaving, particularly, it is the construction that makes the pattern. Therefore, a thorough knowledge of the kinds of fabric structures is essential if the weaver is to avoid the monotony that inevitably comes from limiting to one or two the fabric constructions used.

An artist can paint a picture with only red, yellow, blue, white and black on his palette, but rarely does he do so. The palette will contain several shades of red, of blue, of green, and of still other colors. So it is with the weaver. One might weave for years without exhausting the possibilities of a 1-2-3-4 threading, but it would get very tiresome without some variety to add spice to the work.

At the beginning of the revival of interest in handweaving in the early part of this century, the type of weave used most often was that which we know today as Colonial overshot. That and the twills were the sum total of our knowledge of weaves. We used the overshot for everything whether it was suitable or not; it was all that we had. Later, other weaves were added to the weaver's repertoire, but we were still thinking in terms of "patterns." Inevitably some patterns became hackneyed and all pattern weaving came to have a look of sameness.

It was in the 1940's that the reaction to pattern became most violent. It was then too that yarn manufacturers began to make novelty yarns available to handweavers for the first time. "Pattern" became a style of weaving that was definitely passé. The then new style came to depend for interest on color and texture entirely. Tabby and twill were the only weaves used, and the coarser the better. "Texture weavers" had a tendency to speak disparagingly of "pattern weavers." This, of course, was utter nonsense. Every fabric has pattern and it just as truly has texture. The pattern of taffeta certainly is subordinate to its texture, but the close orderly arrangement of warp and weft is as truly pattern as the most elaborate arrangement in Grandma's coverlet; and the smooth even crispness is as much texture as is the roughness of tweed or upholstery.

With a craft as old as weaving it is difficult to find anything really new. The new things are actually old ones in different forms. No matter how hard one tries to be original, sooner or later someone else appears with the same "original" idea. Particularly this is true of four-harness weaving, and it is true because of the mechanics of the loom. For painting or sculpture, the artist may derive his inspiration from anywhere. For a tapestry or other pictorial weaving, the field is also wide. But to create a fabric in which pattern and texture are in proper balance, the weaver must choose designs which conform to the mechanical limitations of the loom. Various types of fabrics have their own sets of limitations and rules governing their production. If these limitations are known and understood, designing becomes easy and its field is widened. To do original weaving, there is no substitute for a thorough knowledge of the techniques of handweaving.

It is to analyze and explain the mechanical limitations governing the production of various fabrics; to show their distinguishing characteristics; to show how they are related to each other and how they differ from each other, that this book is written. It is not the intention to present new patterns and drafts, or even a collection of weaves and patterns not so new, but to show that though the pattern itself is not always so important, what is done with the pattern makes for original design in handweaving.

There are many classifications of weaving. These vary according to the classifier and the purpose for which the classification is made. A splendid classification of fabrics in general is found in *Fabrics and How to Know Them* by Grace Denny (J. B. Lippincott). It covers the entire field of fabrics from the merchandising standpoint. A very scientific classification is Nancy Andrews Reath's *The Weaves of Handloom Fabrics* (Pennsylvania Museum). This includes all types of weaves from the earliest and simplest through the brocades of ancient China and Persia and the velvets of Italy and France to the beginning of the industrial era.

For modern handweavers there are two general types of pattern weaving: (1) finger-controlled, sometimes called "art weaving" in the Scandinavian countries, and (2) harness-controlled. It is with the harness-controlled patterns that we are here concerned and, for the most part, with patterns for four-harness looms. If the essentials of four-harness fabrics are understood by the weaver, it is an easy step to the use of multi-harness looms.

The outline as given here is chosen because each type of fabric, or weave, has certain characteristics of appearance and structure that set it apart from every other type. Each type may be varied almost indefinitely; it is the variation that makes for originality in weaving.

OUTLINE OF FABRICS FROM THE STANDPOINT OF STRUCTURE

TABBY or plain weave may be varied by changing the color or size or texture of the yarns used, or by a combination of these.

TWILLS

> Direct (right or left)
> Point (herringbone or irregular)
> Broken
> Repeat

M'S AND O'S (a form of twill)

The BRONSONS

> Spot
> Lace

SUMMER-AND-WINTER

CRACKLE or JAMTLANDSVAV

COLONIAL OVERSHOT

Pattern is quite apart from structure, and it is possible to weave a given pattern in two or more of the various weaves. It is possible also to make variations in all of them until they lose all resemblance to the old coverlet type of weaving that has dominated much of American handweaving for so long.

This book is not concerned with the general mechanics of the loom—it presupposes a knowledge of dressing and gating a loom. It is for those weavers who know how to manage the action of their looms and who wish to make those looms do their bidding in producing the fabrics which their imaginations envision.

CHAPTER 1

Cloth Diagrams

A *cloth diagram* is a sort of blueprint of the finished cloth.

A *cloth analysis* consists of the cloth diagram together with its drafts.

A *draft* is the written directions for weaving a given piece of cloth. It consists of threading draft, tie-up, and treadling draft.

A *threading draft* is the diagram which shows the order in which the warp threads are drawn through the heddles. There are many ways of writing threading drafts, but the one most commonly used in the United States is written on cross-section (graph) paper with each black square representing one warp thread. Usually the bottom row of squares represents the first or front harness, and the top row of squares represents the back or fourth harness (Fig. 1).

A *tie-up* shows which harnesses are used in any combination. With four harnesses, there are six possible combinations of two: 1 and 2; 2 and 3; 3 and 4; 4 and 1; 1 and 3; 2 and 4. These six combinations are generally known as the *standard tie-up*. If only one harness is used at a time, this is usually known as a *single tie-up*. Any other combination of harnesses is known as an *irregular tie-up*.

1

A *treadling draft* shows the order in which the combinations of harnesses are used to produce a given design. As generally written, it looks like a threading draft in a vertical position. Each black square represents one weft thread used with the treadle indicated directly below it in the tie-up.

Before attempting to make original designs it is necessary to know thoroughly how to make a cloth diagram. This not only makes it possible to detect errors in the draft, but also enables the designer to see where changes may or may not be an improvement.

PROCEDURE

The threading draft is written across the paper horizontally, either at the top or at the bottom of the page. There are advocates of both positions, but in this book the drafts will be written at the bottom of the page. This seems to correspond a little more closely to the position of weaving on the loom and is usually less confusing to beginners. On the loom, as the weaving progresses by entering the weft threads and beating them into place, the web grows in the direction away from the weaver as he sits at the loom. So, if the paper is placed in front of one on a table-top, and one starts plotting the diagram from the bottom, the work will grow just as the actual weaving grows.

As an example, take the familiar rosepath pattern. The threading draft is written across the bottom of the sheet (Fig. 1). The tie-up is for the combination of harnesses 1 and 3 and the combination of 2 and 4. The treadling draft (the vertical column to the right) calls for the alternate use of these two combinations.

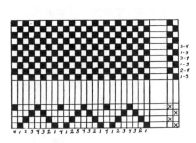

Figure 1

Each row of squares in a vertical line represents a warp thread drawn through the eye of a heddle on the harnesses as shown in the threading draft below. In the analysis the squares representing visible warp threads are left white and the squares representing visible weft threads are blacked in.

In actual weaving on the loom, when the #1 and #3 harnesses are lowered, the weft thread passes over every warp thread on harness 1 and harness 3. Similarly, in the diagram, the first weft thread calls for the combination of 1 and 3, and to show that a weft thread is on top of these #1 and #3 warp threads, every square above a 1 and a 3 is filled in with black. The second weft thread calls for the combination of 2 and 4, and all squares above the 2's and 4's of the threading draft are filled in with black. Working each successive row of horizontal squares to show a black weft thread crossing a white warp thread, one makes a diagram analysis of plain tabby weave.

In some textbooks for industrial weaving, the combinations of the tie-up refer to harnesses that rise and are called "risers"; the opposite harnesses are called "sinkers." In the diagrams, the sinkers are blacked in. The result is the same, but the method is less direct. This industrial method more nearly fits hand looms with rising sheds.

In Fig. 2, still with the rosepath threading, the tie-up is changed to the standard twill tie-up, and the treadling is a straight twill. On the loom, harnesses 1 and 2 are tied to the first treadle; 2 and 3 to the second treadle; 3 and 4 to the third, and 4 and 1 to the fourth. In the treadling draft, the first weft thread calls for the use of the first treadle or the 1—2 combination. In the analysis, the horizontal row of squares even with this first weft thread is worked first (shown on the diagram as row a to a'). In this row, every square that is above a 1 and a 2 of the threading draft is filled in with black to show that in the weaving the black weft thread passes over the 1's and 2's

Figure 2

of the white warp. Row b to b' is worked next, and the treadling draft calls for the use of all 2's and all 3's. Every square on row b—b' that is above a 2 and a 3 of the warp draft is blacked in. Similarly, row c—c' is worked for all 3's and 4's, and row d—d' is worked for 4's and 1's. Row e—e' goes back to the 1—2 combination, and is exactly like row a—a'; row f—f' is like row b—b', and so on as far as it is desired to carry the diagram.

In the upper part of Fig. 2, the treadling draft has been changed and the resulting pattern is shown. The procedure is the same as with the straight twill.

Fig. 3 shows one of the less well-known huck weaves. The threading draft, at first glance, bears a resemblance to the Monk's Belt pattern; the tie-up is irregular (two of the pedals are tied for tabby and the other two are tied to *three* harnesses each); there is nothing unusual in the treadling draft. The procedure for plotting the diagram is the same as for tabby weave. The first weft thread passes over the warp threads on *three* harnesses instead of two as in the previous diagrams, so that the squares above 1, 3, and 4 are blacked in.

In making a diagram analysis, one finds it much easier to cover the squares according to the numbers shown in the tie-up than to transpose and cover those *not* shown. On a loom with

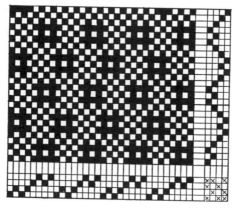

Figure 3

a falling shed, if the treadling is followed as given in the treadling draft, the resulting cloth will show on the visible side of the web exactly as drawn in the diagram. If a loom with a rising shed is used, the *under side* of the web will be the same as the diagram. Regardless of rising or falling shed, in order to turn the under side of a fabric to the top or visible side while weaving, transpose the treadling to the opposite combinations.

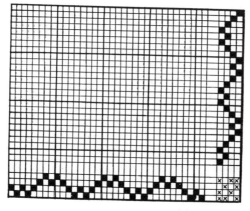

Figure 4

That is, instead of treadling 1—2, treadle 3—4; instead of 2—3, treadle 1—4; instead of 3—4, treadle 2—3; and instead of 1—4, treadle its opposite of 2—3.

PROBLEM
Work out the analysis for the draft given in Fig. 4.

CHAPTER 2

Cloth Analysis

As it is necessary to be able to plot a cloth diagram from a given draft, so it is necessary to be able to reverse the process and find the draft for a given piece of cloth, in order to have a full understanding of its structure and classification.

PROCEDURE

For a beginning, choose a cloth of a rather coarse yarn and of a two-thread construction, preferably one with a contrasting color in warp and weft. Fig. 5 shows such a piece; it was woven on a 16-dent reed of carpet warp—white warp, orange weft. The threads are large enough to be seen easily and the pattern is obvious and easily followed.

First, determine if possible which is warp and which is weft. If there is a selvage on the piece, there can be no doubt about it. If there is no selvage, the construction of the threads themselves may give the clue; or perhaps the general appearance of the cloth will tell the story. If the two yarns are different, it is likely that the stronger one is the warp. The pattern, if taken into consideration with the intended use of the cloth, may tell which is warp; for example, in apparel fabrics, stripes are usu-

Figure 5

ally in the warp direction. Naturally there can be no hard and fast rule. If it is impossible to tell which is warp and which is weft, one set of threads will have to be arbitrarily designated as warp, and the diagram made accordingly.

Draw out a warp thread and a weft thread or ravel out two adjacent edges to make a straight and even beginning for counting the threads. If the piece of cloth cannot be cut or a thread drawn, sew a thread of contrasting color along a single warp thread and a single weft. The diagram at Fig. 6 was made from the illustration at Fig. 5. Beginning at the lower right-hand corner of the cloth, take the first weft thread and count its steps as it passes under and over the white warps. In the photograph, the first weft thread passes over one, under three, over three, under two, over two, and so on. As the thread is counted, the squares are marked on squared paper, one black square for a visible weft; three squares are left white to indicate visible warps. Continue across the row, marking black squares for visible wefts and leaving a white square for every visible warp. Make the diagram wide enough for at least two repeats of the pattern. When the first thread is finished across the width of the paper, count the second thread in the same way. *Be sure* to start every weft thread at the same warp. The second weft thread in the sample and in the diagram reads under two, over one, under two, over one, under two, over two, and so on. Continue until the diagram includes two repeats of the pattern. Usually after the first six or eight weft threads have been carefully counted, the pattern is obvious enough for carrying on the diagram without counting every thread or further raveling.

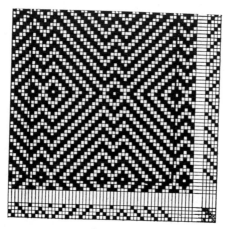

Figure 6

When the diagram is complete, choose one repeat of the pattern and mark a line around it. The enclosing lines may begin at any warp or any weft thread. The resulting drafts may vary slightly in appearance according to which square is chosen as the beginning one.

The choice of a beginning in Fig. 6 is easy. The design is obviously a twill. The beginning lines at the bottom and at the right edges of the repeat are placed at the threads where the twills reverse themselves, and thus make a logical beginning. The enclosing line is carried around the four sides of one complete pattern repeat.

TO FIND THE DRAFT

If you begin at the lower corner and read to the left, the first square on the diagram represents the first warp thread of the draft. It may be on any one of the four harnesses but the logical beginning is harness 1. Therefore let the first warp thread be on the first harness; and to show this, fill in the first square of the warp draft directly below the first square of the diagram. In the cloth diagram, the first square is black, indicating that a

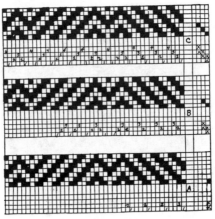

Figure 7

weft thread is on top of a warp thread. The second square is also black; so it is natural to presume that this first row is either the 1—2 or the 1—4 combination. In the interest of consecutive counting, let it be the 1—2 combination. Mark 1—2 on the tie-up and fill in the first square of the treadling draft—this first square will be directly above the 1—2 of the tie-up. Mark across the row all those squares which are apparently 1 and 2 on the draft. It is well to do this with pencil and lightly, for in an irregular pattern it is often necessary to make changes (see A of Fig. 7).

In the second row of the cloth diagram, the first square is white, a warp thread; it is established as #1 on the draft. The second and third squares are black, or weft squares. Since the second square is established as #2, this row must be the 2—3 combination, and is so marked on the tie-up and on the treadling draft. At the bottom of the draft, 2's and 3's are penciled in (See B of Fig. 7).

In the third row of the diagram, the first and second squares are white; they are established as #1 and #2 on the draft. The third and fourth squares are black or visible wefts. And since the third space is established as #3 on the draft, the fourth must be #4, and this third row must be the 3—4 combination. It is so marked on the tie-up and on the treadling draft. The 3's and 4's are penciled in on the threading draft below all black squares of the third row of the cloth diagram (see C of Fig. 7).

The 1—4 combination is the only one not yet used; so the fourth row of the diagram is assumed to be that combination in order to use it as a check on the other rows of the draft. If there are no conflicts in the numbered draft as written in pencil, the threading draft may be written in the conventional way at the bottom of the diagram. Fig. 7 shows the separate steps of writing the draft. Only the lower rows of the cloth diagram are shown. It now remains only to count the repeats of the treadling draft and to determine on which combinations the treadling reverses itself.

If a different starting point is chosen, the resulting draft may have a different appearance, but the draft itself is just as correct as the result obtained at Fig. 6. This is illustrated in Fig. 8. Rosepath has been chosen because of brevity, but any draft

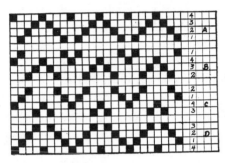

Figure 8

may be changed in the same way. At A the draft is written in the usual manner. At B, the #1 harness has been taken bodily and placed in the #4 position, thus giving the first line to the #2 harness. The same sort of transposition has been made at C and again at D. Four different-appearing drafts are the result. If a straight twill treadling is used, the resulting fabrics are

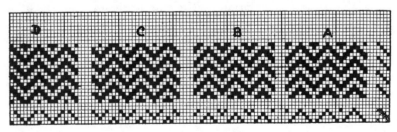

Figure 9

Figure 10

identical, though starting at different points of the pattern (Fig. 9). If a reverse twill treadling is used, the resulting fabrics will be slightly different. If the treadling draft is shifted as the threading draft was, the results will be identical. If A is treadled 1—2, 2—3, 3—4, 3—2, 1—2, 2—3, and so on, in order to get the same cloth B must be treadled 1—4, 1—2, 2—3, 3—4, 3—2, 1—2, 1—4, 1—2, and so on. Similarly, C must start with 3—4 and D must start with 2—3.

Fig. 10 shows a novelty weave similar to the commercially known waffle weave. The cloth is woven 20 ends to the inch of a soft crochet cotton yarn generally known as bedspread cotton. The warp is white and the weft is rose.

When analyzed upon cross-section paper as described at the beginning of this chapter, the diagram appears as shown at Fig. 11. There is nothing about this diagram to suggest a twill,

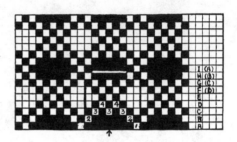

Figure 11

but the repeats of the pattern are plainly visible. There are eight warp threads in one repeat, and it would be natural to assume that there have been eight harnesses used for this fabric. On further study, however, it is seen that this is a bilateral design with the warp thread at the arrow (Fig. 11) as the vertical axis. The second ·(left) half of the draft must be the reverse of the first (right) half. This disposes of the eight-harness idea, and leaves to be decided only whether four or five harnesses have been used.

Now to consider the weft threads. There are eight threads in the weft repeat and it too is a bilateral design. The pattern reverses on rows A and E. E is the center or horizontal axis of this repeat. Rows F and D are alike; G and C are alike; H and B are alike. This leaves A and E as the only rows in the repeat not duplicated, and these are reversing rows. The fact that there are five different rows, three of which are repeated in a single unit of the pattern, establishes without a doubt that there are five pedals, or combinations of harnesses, used. It would appear that the treadling draft is an even point twill.

TO FIND THE THREADING DRAFT

Go back to the diagram (Fig. 11) and first consider *row* A. Let the first square to the right, in the designated repeat, represent the warp thread on the #1 harness. It is the only visible warp on this row and tells two important stories: (a) there is only one #1 harness thread in the repeat of the pattern, and (b) the first combination of harnesses in the tie-up calls for the use of all harnesses except #1.

Row B. The first square on the right is established as representing the warp on the #1 harness. The second square can be a #2. It is a visible warp thread, as is the last square in that row. Since this is a bilateral design, both of these squares then will be placed on #2 harness. In the tie-up for this row #2 will be the only harness not used, and, therefore, all harnesses except #2 make the second combination of the tie-up.

Row C. Still reading from the right, make the first square #1 and the second #2. The third space, like the first one, is a visible warp. It cannot be a #1, for if it were, it would have been visible also in row A. Therefore, it must be considered as a warp on #3 harness, as is also its corresponding warp on the left of the pattern—the second space from the left enclosing line. In this row C, the warp threads on #1 and #3 are visible and so is the center or axis thread. The center thread cannot be on the #1 harness, for it was not visible on row A. Therefore, it must be on #3 also. In the tie-up for this row, #1 and #3 are the harnesses *not* used.

Row D. In this row, there are three black squares; the weft thread passes over three warp threads which have just been identified as on the #3 harness. The tie-up for this row calls for the use of the third harness only.

Row E. This is the center row of the repeat. The weft thread passes over only two warp threads, those on each side of the center thread of the repeat. They are the only two warp threads that have not been placed on a harness, and since harnesses 1, 2 and 3 have been used, these two remaining warps must of necessity be on harness 4. Thus we find that this is a four-harness draft. It might have been a five-harness draft with the center or axis warp on the fifth harness, but the diagram makes no call for use of this center thread by itself, and it is undoubtedly on the third harness.

With the threading draft completed, it remains only to finish the treadling draft and to write the tie-up. For the tie-up, the first combination calls for the use of all but the first harness; therefore the first combination is 2—3—4. In row B, the #2 harness is the only one not used; so that combination on the tie-up becomes 1—3—4. Row C calls for the use of harnesses 2 and 4; so that combination of the tie-up is 2—4. Row D calls for the use of #3 only, and row E calls for the use of #4 only. The complete draft is shown at Fig. 12.

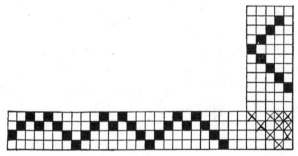

Figure 12

A dishcloth found on the housewares counter of a five-and-ten-cent store one day offered a challenge to a weaver. This cloth was a grand problem for analysis; it was an entirely unfamiliar weave so far as technique was concerned, a very even waffle weave, and alike on both sides, as the cloth at Fig. 10 is not; it had a selvage; the warp and weft threads were practically the same, and coarse enough to be seen easily; the weave was quite loose so that counting was easy. The analysis as shown at Fig. 13 looked very well, but called for five harnesses. The treadling draft, however, called for only four combinations of harnesses or four treadles. Here was a chance for an experiment.

Figure 13   Figure 14

The treadling draft was moved down to become the threading draft, and the threading draft was made the treadling draft. The tie-up was carefully transposed and a new diagram made (Fig. 14).

To prove that this transposition was practical as well as possible, a loom was set up. A six-strand untwisted spun silk was used on a 16-dent reed, white on three harnesses and blue on #4 harness. The weft was all blue. The finished fabric had no need to be ashamed of its plebeian origin. The fact that threading and treadling drafts are interchangeable—providing, of course, that the tie-up is made to conform—is of enormous value in designing, and one that is too often overlooked.

The piece of cloth shown at Fig. 15 is a sample of cotton suiting from a department store, and is a piece which makes a good problem in analysis. There is no selvage on the piece; the warp and weft yarns are identical; and the weave is so even

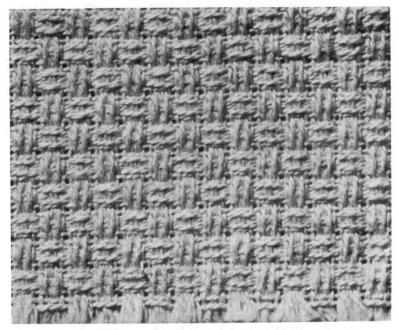

Figure 15

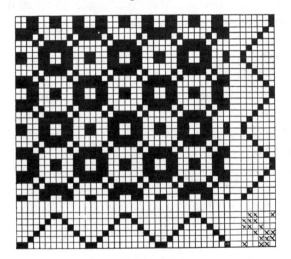

Figure 16

that there is no apparent difference in the length and the breadth of the cloth. The diagram (Fig. 16) proves to be a very interesting pattern, though on paper it looks more like linoleum than basket weave. It is reversing in design, having very definite horizontal and vertical axes. These axes are not threads, as is often the case, but spaces between threads. The resulting draft shows two threads next to each other on the #1 and the #6 harnesses. This oddity does not disturb a handweaver in the least, but it is not the sort of thing that is usually found in commercial weaving. This particular piece of weaving was most likely done on a twelve-harness dobby loom, threaded (or "drawn," in mill parlance) to a straight twill. A straight twill is used extensively in commercial weaving because of its possibilities; with such a threading it is a comparatively easy matter to change a dobby-chain. The twelve-harness draft is given at Fig. 17.

Regardless of how many harnesses have been used in weaving any piece of cloth, the method of analysis is the same: (1) determine warp and weft, if possible; (2) mark definite warp and weft threads to count; (3) make a diagram on cross-section paper, letting a black square represent a visible weft thread and leaving a white square to represent a visible warp thread; (4) mark one repeat of the pattern on the diagram; (5) beginning at the lower right-hand corner of the diagram, let the first square

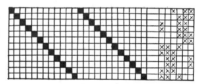

Figure 17

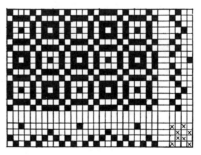

Figure 18

Figure 19

represent the warp thread on the #1 harness; (6) read to the left and up, in a diagonal direction.

Fig. 18 shows an attempt to reduce the design of Fig. 16 to a four-harness weave. The resulting cloth is shown at Fig. 19.

PROBLEMS

1. Write the draft for Fig. 20.
2. Write an analysis for a piece of cloth, the draft of which is familiar.
3. Make an analysis for a piece of cloth woven by you far enough in the past that the draft is not familiar, but which is available for checking.
4. Make an analysis of a piece of commercially woven cloth.

Figure 20

CHAPTER 3

Tabby and
Its Variations

In tabby, taffeta, or plain weave—various names for the simplest type of fabric—each warp thread passes alternately over one weft and under one weft; each weft thread passes alternately under one warp thread and over one warp. In spite of this simple structure, considerable variation is possible in tabby without changing the essential characteristic of the weave.

When the same yarn is used for both warp and weft and the number of ends (warp threads) per inch is equal to the number of picks (weft threads) per inch, the fabric is said to be woven square. If a heavier warp is used with a finer weft, the weft is more prominent and the fabric, while still a taffeta weave, becomes a rep fabric. If a very fine warp is sleyed closely and if the weft is coarse, the warp is more prominent, and the ribs of the fabric are crosswise rather than lengthwise and the fabric comes within the general classification of faille. Tapestries generally are in the rep class, and the ordinary rag rug is in the faille class.

To do justice to designing in the field of plain weave would take a volume in itself; therefore this chapter can be merely an outline. Designs for plain weave depend principally upon color, which is a matter of personal taste, and upon variety of yarn, which is a matter of what is on the market.

Plain weave may be varied by (1) changing the proportion of warp to weft, (2) the use of various kinds and sizes of yarns, (3) the use of color, and (4) combining any two or all three of the preceding methods.

When two weft threads pass over two warp threads and under the next two warps, and on the following row pass under two and over two, the resulting cloth is tabby in technique, but becomes basket weave in texture and appearance. And basket weave has many variations. Monk's cloth is, perhaps, the most familiar example of basket weave. In this cloth two or more threads are used as one, but between each group of threads is a single thread to act as a tie and to give the cloth more stability. The group of threads weaves as a single thread and the over-one-under-one characteristic is not impaired.

In monk's cloth all yarns are the same size. Another interesting tabby variation is the alternation of one or two heavy yarns with one or more fine yarns, each yarn single through the heddle eye, but the fine ones doubled in the reed. This is a simple variation and known to all weavers, but the many arrangements possible have never been exhausted and probably never will be so long as there is a weaver living who has a creative urge. It is sometimes hard to know where changing proportion ends and varying size of yarn begins. The fabric known commercially as dimity is an example of this. At regular intervals a heavier warp thread is introduced to make lengthwise stripes; if the heavy thread is used in the weft as well, the result is cross-bar dimity.

Alternating a group of very elastic yarns (such as wool) with a group of very stable yarns (such as rayon) in the warp will produce a seersucker effect. In any warp where there is a difference in size of yarns, great care must be taken in beaming. Tension is all important, whether it is meant to be even or not.

Mixing the types of yarn is almost as much a matter of what is available as it is a matter of imagination. The so-called novelty yarns are sometimes hard to find, or may be of the bumpy type that presents difficulties in the reed. With such yarns a coarse reed with several threads through each dent will probably work better than a finer one that may break or wear

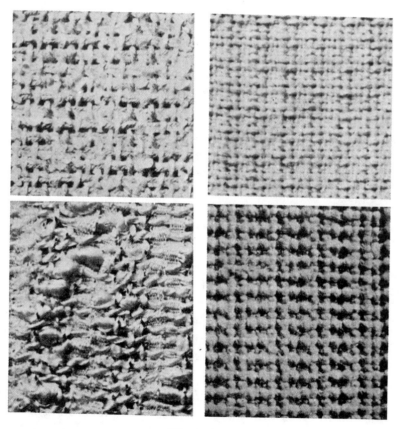

Figure 21

the warp. Dull yarns and shiny yarns, rough yarns and smooth yarns, coarse yarns and fine yarns—how to use them is mostly a matter of imagination and courage. An inventive weaver has imagination enough to see the possibilities in the string the butcher uses or the soft cord the gardener knows as "grape-cord" or the things that nobody ever heard of using on a loom, combined with the love of experimenting for new effects. Combine several kinds and types—make dozens of samples. Out of a dozen pieces one may be really good, the others fair to poor. But even one really exciting combination from a hundred attempts is worth the effort. The designing of texture weaves in tabby cannot be taught—it has to be learned; and the only way to learn it is to do it. A very few suggestions are shown in Fig. 21.

An even greater variety of pattern is made possible by the use of color. A very good beginning exercise in the use of color is to make a sample blanket. It is easier to do this on the loom than on paper; the results leave less to the imagination and the finished blanket is well worth the effort. Two colors used in different proportions, or several pairs of different colors used in the same proportion, will produce fascinating results. Many of the amazing checks and plaids so common in men's suiting are the result of color placement in warp and weft.

Fig. 22 is a photograph of a sample blanket. In this blanket only two colors were used: tan and brown. Two ends and two picks of a contrasting color were added to separate the various samples. The threading draft for color is given at Fig. 23. The weft colors follow the same sequence as the warp colors.

Color in weaving can be a very uncertain quantity. Because two colors look well together in the skein is no guarantee they will weave well together, and often colors which fight each other in the skein will mix in the fabric to produce a glorious tone. It is one thing to combine *areas* of color but quite another

Figure 22

Figure 23

to *mix* those colors. A rainbow blanket will teach many things about the idiosyncracies of color. Use No. 20 perle cotton, which can be obtained in a vast range of color and when sleyed at 32 per inch will weave nearly square. With the colors use black, gray and white. Next to the black, gray and white arrange the colors in their rainbow sequence of red, orange, yellow, green, blue and violet. Make the warp at least three yards long and have one and one-half to two inches of each color. Set up the loom in a plain twill so that one blanket can be woven in tabby and one in twill. Weave with the same colors so that each color sample is approximately square. Keep the beat even so that there are the same number of wefts per inch as warps per inch.

Note that where the black weft crosses the black warp, black results; where black weft crosses gray warp, the resulting gray is darker than the gray warp, and where black crosses white, gray is the result. The black weft will make all the colors darker and more "dead" than the warp; the gray weft will dull all the colors and the white weft will make them lighter. Red crossing black should result in the same tone as black crossing red. The color is not affected when red crosses red, but when it crosses orange an entirely new color—red-orange—is produced. When red crosses yellow, orange is the result, but red across green is nondescript. On the loom, red weft on yellow warp may look quite different from yellow weft on red warp. If the sample was woven square, however, this difference will not be nearly so noticeable when the work is taken off the loom and washed.

Make one complete sample in tabby and one in twill. Then re-sley the warp to 40 per inch and weave another blanket. Here the warps will be closer together and more prominent than the wefts. The result will be quite different from the blanket sleyed at 32 per inch. A third pair of blankets can be made by sleying at 24 per inch to make the weft more prominent. These color blankets are fun to do and furnish valuable reference material.

The use of color in the warp or weft to make striped material needs no explanation. If stripes are used in both warp and weft, the resulting pattern is plaid. Scottish tartans are marvelous examples of good plaids. The proportions are pleasing and a great variety of distinctive patterns is obtained from the use of a few colors. The tartan palette consists of red, green, blue, yellow, black and white. Some of the plaids developed since 1800 have introduced magenta and light blue, but these are not nearly so pleasing as the standard patterns which have developed through many years of use.

When samples for texture effect and sample blankets for color have been made, it should not be difficult to combine color and texture into interesting fabrics.

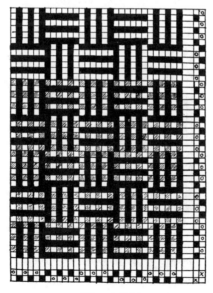

Figure 24

For those who wish to experiment with tabby patterns on paper, Fig. 24 will explain the procedure. The cloth diagram of tabby weave is penciled in lightly (diagonal lines in Fig. 24) for the visible wefts. After the entire cloth diagram is made, refer to the indicated color in the draft, and where black warp is visible, fill in that square with black ink; where black weft is visible, fill in that square. After all colors have been inked in, erase the pencil marks to see the effect of the pattern. Fig. 24 is the familiar Log Cabin.

Fig. 25 is a simple problem in three-color designing. A two-color warp is arranged in sequence of two browns (represented by black squares) and three beige (represented by small circles). The check marks indicate the visible wefts, regardless of color. They have been marked over the first eight warps only, to avoid confusion in the diagram. The first seven wefts are beige. Because they will show as a stripe, the brown warps are inked in. This is not too interesting a pattern.

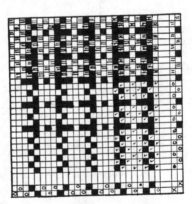

Figure 25

Next the treadling is changed to one brown and three beige. The pairs of brown warps will continue to be visible just as before, and they can be inked in to begin with. Then the brown wefts will be inked in over the check marks or penciled squares in those rows where a visible brown weft is indicated. After two repeats of one brown and three beige, tan is substituted for the beige and represented by horizontal lines. The fundamental pattern is not changed, but color quality is quite different.

Colored pencils, water colors, or colored ink are more interesting to work with than black-and-white lines. The only drawback to the color system is that the pencil marks of the original diagram cannot be erased and will show through the transparent colors. After some practice, it should be possible to work without the pencil skeleton.

PROBLEM
Complete Fig. 26.

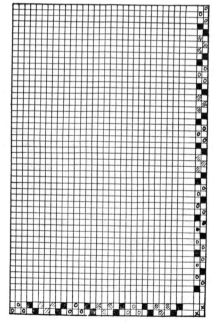

Figure 26

CHAPTER 4

Twills and
Their Variations

Twill, according to the dictionary, is "an appearance of diagonal lines or ribs produced in textile fabrics by passing the weft thread over one and under two threads instead of over one and under the next." But Mr. Webster leaves out the most important part of the definition, or perhaps he just expects us to know that "over one" is always over the warp thread immediately next to the warp that was "overed" in the preceding row. And the inference is that the weft is always over one warp, whereas it can be over several warps as well as under two or more.

Twills form the largest family of weaving patterns and are ancestors of nearly all types of pattern weaving, except perhaps the brocades. Twills require a minimum of three harnesses, but may be made on almost any number. However, a set-up of more than twenty harnesses is not very practical, even on power looms. For the purposes of this book, four-harness twills will be given primary attention.

Twills are divided according to their form into (a) direct, (b) point, (c) broken, and (d) repeat twills. The threading drafts for these are shown at Figs. 27, 39, and 40, and the cloth diagram made for twelve picks in a direct twill treadling for the direct, point, and broken twills in Fig. 27.

A *direct twill* is one in which the direction of the slant or twill does not change. If the treadling is in a direct twill also, the direction of the twill is perfectly obvious. Direct twills are divided into "right" and "left" twills depending upon the direction of the slant. Although only four harnesses are shown in Fig. 27, these classifications hold good for any number of harnesses.

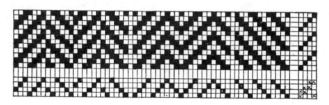

Figure 27

To make twill designs, the number of threads in one repeat (corresponding to the number of harnesses) *must* be broken up into an *even* number of component parts. On four harnesses, $2 + 2$ and $1 + 3$ are the only possible combinations. When the number of harnesses is increased, the possibilities of arrangement are also greater. More patterns are possible on a five-harness loom than on a four, and more are possible on a six than on a five.

On a six-harness loom there are six threads in a repeat of a direct twill, and six may be broken up as follows:

$6 = 3 + 3$ $6 = 2 + 1 + 2 + 1$
$6 = 2 + 4$ $6 = 3 + 1 + 1 + 1$
$6 = 1 + 5$ $6 = 2 + 2 + 1 + 1$

In the first group of arrangements there are two parts which added together give six, and in the second group there are four parts in each arrangement.

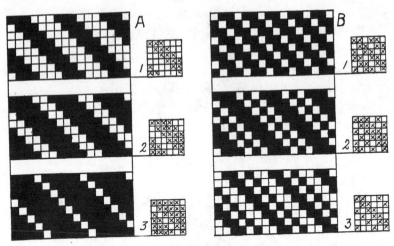

Figure 28

In the first twill the weave is over three and under three. On squared paper make three black squares in a horizontal row and leave three white. Repeat across the row three or more times. In a direct twill the grouping of the warp threads is the same in every pick, but the group as a whole moves to the right or left by one warp thread. On the diagram the second row of squares will start with one white square and continues with three black and three white. Make the diagram ten or twelve squares high. As worked out in the diagram at Fig. 28A, there is nothing particularly interesting about it. It is quite similar to the simple four-harness twill. When woven it would be a closer and heavier fabric than the four-harness one, but would differ little in appearance.

Fig. 28A2 is only slightly more interesting to look upon and would weave not very differently. A3 is really a sateen weave if correctly beaten. If woven square, it would make a flimsy and shapeless piece of cloth.

The first combination of the B group is over two, under one, over two, and under one. The procedure for working the diagram is the same as for the first group. Make two black (over) squares, one white (under), and so on; in each succeeding row the black squares are slipped one square to the left. This is a denim twill and might just as well be woven on a three-harness loom. B2 and B3 make twills that weave well and are pleasing to the eye. B3 has more interest and better balance. With the diagrams made, the tie-ups are obvious.

The making of twill designs is not the most practical designing, for most handweavers use only four harnesses, but it is a splendid exercise in simple design and is fascinating to do. With an increased number of harnesses, the possibilities multiply rapidly. For example:

$$12 = 4 + 2 + 4 + 2 \qquad\qquad 12 = 3 + 3 + 2 + 2 + 1 + 1$$
$$12 = 4 + 4 + 2 + 2 \qquad\qquad 12 = 3 + 2 + 1 + 3 + 2 + 1$$
$$12 = 3 + 3 + 4 + 2 \qquad\qquad 12 = 2 + 1 + 1 + 1 + 4 + 3$$

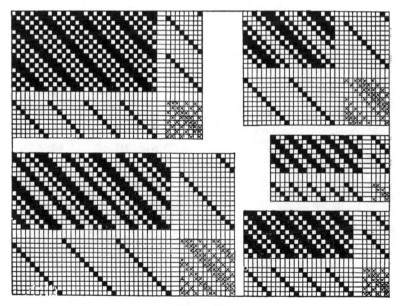

Figure 29

And these are only the beginning of the even number of combinations that when added together make twelve.

Fig. 29 shows a few suggestions for combinations for four-, six-, eight-, ten-, and twelve-harness twills.

Point twills are those twills in which the direction of slant reverses at stated intervals. If the point occurs at regular intervals so that the amount of slant is the same in each direction, the point twill is known as a herringbone twill. All herringbone twills are point twills, but all point twills are not herringbone twills. In Fig. 27 the broken twill is also a herringbone twill.

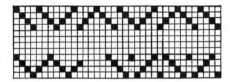

Figure 30

Figure 31

The simplest point twill is 1-2-3-4-3-2-1-2-3-4-3-2, the direction of the twill changing on 1 and 4, or at every third thread. The width of the stripe or the size of the herringbone may be varied as desired by increasing the number of warp threads between the reversing threads; thus 1-2-3-4-1-4-3-2-1-4-1-2-3-4-1-4-3-2-1-4 reverses at every fifth thread (Fig. 30).

If point twills are woven with a direct twill treadling on a standard tie-up, the resulting cloth is a point twill; but if woven with a point twill treadling the cloth has a geometric pattern of the goose-eye type (Fig. 31).

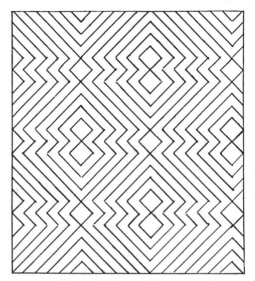

Figure 32

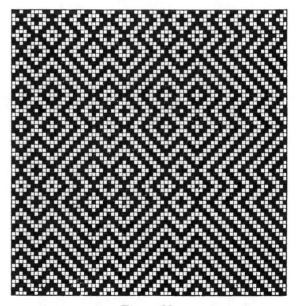

Figure 33

The cloth shown in Fig. 5 is a point twill woven with a point or reversing twill treadling but not as drawn in. Diagramatically, that pattern could be represented as shown in Fig. 32. When the treadling draft is the same as the threading draft, the resulting pattern is Fig. 33.

Point twills may be made to fit a given space or a definite article. For example, a towel in twill weave could be designed so that the diagram would look like Fig. 34, and the draft would

Figure 34

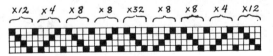

Figure 35

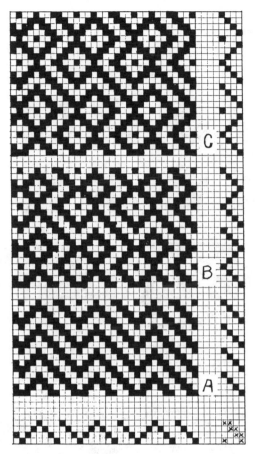

Figure 36

be written as at Fig. 35. This towel calls for 392 ends. If a 40/2 linen warp is used and sleyed at 30 per inch, the towel finishes a little more than 12 inches wide and about 20 inches long in order to have the correct proportions.

Fig. 36 shows an irregular point twill woven in three ways. At A it is woven with a direct twill treadling. At B it is woven as drawn in, but the resulting pattern has a rather one-sided effect and gives the impression of there having been a mistake in the weaving. This apparent fault has been corrected at C by carrying the treadling one pick farther before reversing. This makes the two small squares equal in size and design.

So far, only the standard tie-up has been considered. On

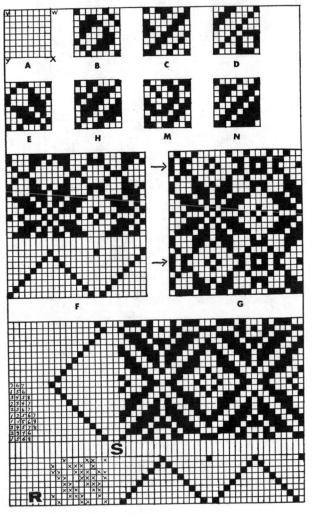

Figure 37

four-harness twills, whether direct or point, the use of an irregular tie-up results not so much in patterns as in texture, and this will be discussed later. However, it is quite possible to make definite designs for point twills on six or more harnesses. The eight-harness rosepath has endless possibilities and is used here to illustrate one simple method of making patterns (Fig. 37). The method is the same no matter how many harnesses are used. The twill may reverse on the same harness each time as in the rosepath type of draft, or it may reverse on the first and last harnesses.

As shown in Fig. 37, on squared paper mark off a space eight squares by eight squares as at A. In this space, fill in squares to make a "key" pattern. Avoid long groups of either black or white squares; usually five is the limit. Place small straight-edged mirrors along the axis V—W and W—X to show the repeat and to suggest desirable changes. In the same way, test the repeat along axes V—Y and X—Y.

Key patterns B, C, and D are not too interesting. When tested with mirrors, the pattern at E gives promise of a somewhat better effect. Using the E pattern, put the draft of rosepath under the key pattern square as at F, and plot out the reverse. There is a #8 thread at the end of the draft; therefore the row of squares above the #8 or the row at the W—X axis will have to be repeated to make the reverse square.

Next fill in the pattern on the V—W axis. The design may now be considered complete or an extra row of weft can be added for the reverse line in order to square the pattern. This is shown at G with arrows marking the reverse lines.

Key pattern H has been worked out at S. With the diagram complete, the next step is to work out the tie-up and treadling. On the first row of pattern (S) it will be seen that there are black squares above harnesses 1, 5, 6, and 8. This then becomes the combination for the first pattern weft or the first combination in the tie-up. Similarly the second row of harnesses and the second tie-up combination is 2, 3, 4, 6. Note that there are ten combinations in the tie-up.

In a design such as that at D, the extra (#8) reversing thread will work better on the V—Y axis than on the W—X one.

Generally speaking, the simpler designs on paper will be more attractive in the woven fabric than the more elaborate patterns. When woven, pattern M is not nearly so good as pattern N, although when developed on paper like the design at S, it may be more interesting. Make dozens of patterns; don't be discouraged if all are not beautiful and if some do not "work." One good design is worth any amount of time and effort, and making them is more fun than working crossword puzzles.

Although the designs described above are bisymmetrical both horizontally and vertically, they need not be so always. The key pattern can be made and reversed on its vertical axis, as is inevitable, but it can be repeated rather than reversed in the treadling. Naturally this will result in a striped rather than an all-over effect, but sometimes there are advantages in stripes. Or the key pattern may be an oblong.

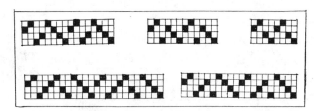

Figure 38

In *broken twill*, as the name implies, continuity is broken. Broken twills are usually point twills and the break occurs at the reverse point. A break in a direct twill appears only as a mistake in the weaving. There may be any number of warps between the reverse or break points—a minimum of two, of course—and the break may occur in any harness (Fig. 38). In Fig. 39, the numbers below the draft indicate the harnesses from which a warp has been omitted to break the continuity.

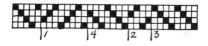

Figure 39

In broken twill no weft thread ever skips more than two warps, while in an ordinary point twill, the weft skips three warps at the reverse points. Compare the diagrams at Fig. 27. Both types have their advantages and disadvantages.

Repeat twill has two consecutive warps repeated two or more times (Fig. 40). This type is seldom used as a twill cloth;

Figure 40   Figure 41

it really belongs in the class of pattern weaving and will be discussed under the heading of Colonial overshot. Repeat twill may be combined with direct twill to give variation (Fig. 41). Care must be taken in the arrangement of this type of twill. Too many repeats too close together will weaken the structure of the fabric. Properly used, it makes an interesting accent.

Variations. Like tabby, twill may also be varied by changing the proportion of warp and weft, by the use of various kinds and sizes of yarns, by the use of color; but most important is the variation that is not possible with tabby, namely the almost endless possibilities in changes of treadling. The texture of cloth may be changed amazingly by changing the treadling. Even with the standard tie-up, varying the order of treadling does wonderful things. For example, any one of the four twill com-

binations alternated with tabby gives a rep effect, and the use
of only three of the four combinations gives a more vertical
illusion than the ordinary weft herringbone (Fig. 42).

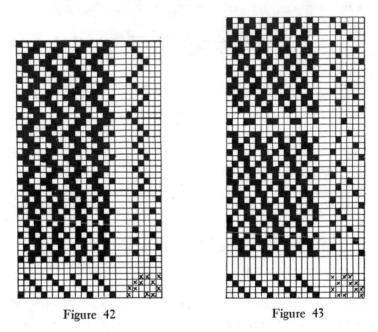

Figure 42   Figure 43

In the combining of tabby with twill alternately, the twill
is elaborated and produces a four-harness version of whipcord
(Fig. 43). Note that the relation of the tabby to the twill makes
quite a difference in the pattern. In the lower part of the diagram, the 1—2 combination is followed by the 2—4 tabby,
while in the upper section the 1—2 combination is followed by
the 1—3 tabby. In actual practice, this is merely the difference
in the two sides of the fabric, regardless of which treadling is
used.

With a point twill the number of potential patterns is more
than doubled. Even the simple and familiar rosepath can keep
any weaver busy for many years.

It is said to have been calculated by some magical mathematical formula that there are 352 variations on the 1-2-3-4 threading. This may be true. One time, I set out to prove or disprove the statement. The results were most interesting. More than 600 possible treadlings were found for the standard tie-up alone. When analyzed on paper, there were dozens of duplications. Some treadlings gave just the opposite side of another treadling (Fig. 43). Without the duplicates, there were found to be 62 basic structures. Of course, most of the 62 could be elaborated almost indefinitely. Eliminated in the treadling as impractical for use were most that gave a warp overshot of more than three picks.

With irregular tie-ups another 50 basic structures were found. These, even more than those on standard tie-ups, could be enlarged and developed endlessly. It is with the irregular tie-ups that one can have the most fun in making designs—and perhaps the most disappointments in weaving them! Generally speaking, irregular tie-ups result in only a crepe effect and the pattern that looks so exciting on paper is lost entirely in the texture. It is by the addition of color and by the use of different yarns that the best results are achieved with these experiments.

Fig. 44 shows the evolution of a design made with an irregular tie-up. Merely as a starting point, the 1—3 tabby was indicated on the diagram for alternate picks, the black squares indicating visible wefts. The 2-3-4 weft was tried first and seemed to be a

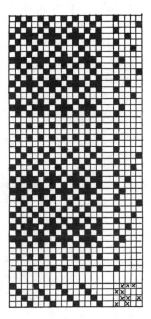

Figure 44

good beginning. The little black cross thus formed suggested that a pattern could be developed by more little crosses and the 1-2-4 weft was next inked in. By this time it became evident that the fabric would be much too unbalanced and weft-faced if these two three-harness combinations continued to alternate. By using the #4 harness alone, the long weft skips were put on the under side of the cloth. Two rows of skips on the under side balanced the cloth, but gave a decidedly horizontal stripe. The design was potentially good, but the treadling needed to be shifted around. When this fabric is woven, the warps give a decidedly diagonal illusion.

Among handweavers there is a large group that uses only tabby and simple twill, the principle being that it is the play of color and texture that distinguishes hand weaving and that pattern weaving belongs in the realm of machine weaving. This attitude may be a bit exaggerated, but the value and importance of color cannot be overemphasized. Take, for example, Fig. 45; if this were woven with a white warp and a black weft, the resulting cloth would be a pepper-and-salt effect on a crepe-like texture—interesting in a mild sort of way. But if both black and white are used in the warp as well as the weft, and arranged as shown in Fig. 46, while the *texture* of the cloth remains the same, the *pattern* becomes most amazingly Chinese Chippendale.

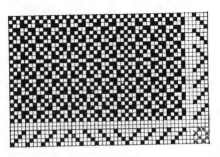

Figure 45

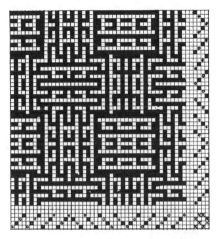

Figure 46

Like the fabric from which Fig. 46 was analyzed, many of the tweeds, and particularly the imported ones that seem to have such astonishing arrangements of lines and diagonals, are merely plain tabby or simple twill in texture, but with very clever color arrangements in both warp and weft.

Making diagrams for color pattern as well as for texture is not so complicated as it may at first seem. The method is explained at Fig. 47. A simple four-harness twill is laid out—threading, tie-up and treadling. In both warp and weft alternate threads are black and the intervening ones are white; this is represented on the draft by black squares and circles respectively.

First the texture is plotted in the regular way, regardless of color, except that instead of filling the squares with solid black to represent visible weft threads, lines of pencil strokes are used. Colored pencils are a great help in this type of designing. Ordinary lead pencil can be used to represent the *structure* of the cloth and later the appropriate colors can be put in. Section A of Fig. 47 shows the texture or weave diagram, regardless of any color that may or may not be used in either warp or weft.

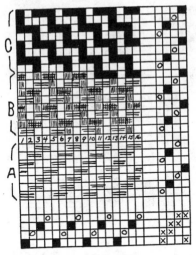

Figure 47

The next step is to superimpose the color on the design. This is shown at B of Fig. 47. The texture marks show clearly which are the visible warps and which are the visible wefts. Begin at the far left and consider the first row of squares, 1 and 2, weft threads. By referring to the treadling draft, you see that this weft thread is white; therefore nothing is done to the first two squares. The third and fourth squares are visible warp threads. Reference to the threading draft at the bottom of the diagram indicates that the third thread is black. (That square is filled in with ink or the properly colored pencil.) The fourth, a warp thread, is white, so the square representing that one is left untouched. In the same manner, 5 and 6, 9 and 10, 13 and 14, are white weft threads; 7, 11 and 15 are black warp threads and the remaining 8, 12 and 16 are white warps. Only squares above 3, 7, 11 and 15 are inked in. Again beginning at the left, consider the second row of squares or what would be the second pick of the fabric. Number 1 is a black warp, 2 and 3 are black weft, and 4 is a white warp. The squares on the diagram which represent black threads, whether warp or weft, are filled in with ink or colored pencil; those squares (4, 8, 12 and 16) which represent visible white warps are left blank. The entire diagram is considered in this way, color being superimposed on the texture diagram. It remains then only to erase the pencil marks and leave the color diagram or pattern, C of Fig.

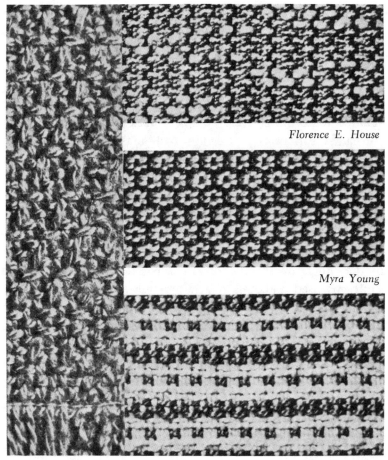

Florence E. House

Myra Young

Berta Harttmann

Figure 48

47. To review: section A of Fig. 47 shows the texture diagram only; B, color and texture; C, color only.

In spite of the tremendous amount of texture weaving being done and its vast importance in today's styles, it is the most difficult type of weaving to write about. No rules can be made for it, nor can it be taught. A few underlying principles can be stated, but the creative work must come from the individual weaver. A weaver with imagination will make good designs in spite of teachers and books, not because of them; and all the books and teachers in the world can't tell the timid soul how to originate fabrics.

Twill is one of the most effective weaves for texture interest. The simple direct twill can be used simply, or it can be adapted to seemingly very complex fabrics—variations in yarn and slight variations in treadling will make a twill look very complicated indeed. A few examples are shown at Fig. 48.

Before leaving twills, it would be well to discuss briefly two valuable uses of the simple 1-2-3-4 twill—namely double-width and double-faced fabrics.

Since only two harnesses are needed for plain or tabby cloth, four harnesses can make two pieces of cloth, one on top of the other, by the use of two separate wefts. If only one shuttle is used and it is used alternately on the top and the bottom fabrics, the two pieces become one fabric in the form of a tube. If one weft is used and two picks are woven on the upper web, then two on the lower one, the resulting fabric becomes a doubled piece with two selvages at one edge of the loom and a fold at the other edge. In double-width fabric, though the threading is a twill, the resulting fabric is a tabby. This fabric like any plain weave may be varied by the use of colored or textured yarns or both.

Because two fabrics are in the reed at one time, the sley must be doubled. A finished fabric of 12 ends per inch must be sleyed in the loom at 24 per inch. Special care must be exercised in the weaving also, for if the edges are pulled in there will be a heavy streak in the middle of the finished piece where the fold occurred on the loom. On the other hand, if there are loops of weft at the fold edge, there will be a sleazy streak through the center of the cloth. Practice will tell how close or how loose to weave the folded edge.

Any two combinations of two harnesses may be used, but the best results are obtained by making one cloth on the #1 and #3 harnesses and the other one on the #2 and #4 harnesses. If #1 and #2 are used against #3 and #4, the fabric will show very definite "reed marks," and the same is true of the #1 and #4 against the #2 and #3 combinations.

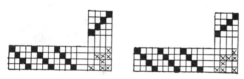

Figure 49

Fig. 49, right, shows the tie-up and treadling for a tubular fabric and, left, the tie-up and treadling for a double-width fabric. Note that it is only the *arrangement* of the tie-up that is diffe'ent in these two instances; in other words, the treadling is changed to make the two different fabrics. Stripes, plaids, and textured fabrics can be done easily and successfully in this way.

Double-faced cloth consists merely of using two colors to weave a weft-faced twill on both sides of a single warp. If a twill is woven by lowering three harnesses at a time, the resulting cloth will be weft-faced on the top and warp-faced on the under side of the web. If only one harness is lowered at a time, the resulting twill is warp-faced on top and weft-faced on the under side. Weaving double-faced cloth, then, is merely a matter of using one color when one harness is lowered and alternating this with the second color when three harnesses are lowered. The only thing to remember is that "opposite" combinations must never be used next to each other. If harness 1 is lowered, the combination of 2-3-4 must *not* follow. The weft skip of three must be allowed to slip over and hide the "over one" of the color used on the under side of the fabric.

The treadling shown at the right of Fig. 50 will give a twill on both sides of the fabric. The treadling may be rearranged to break the twill as shown at the left of Fig. 50.

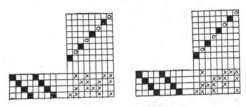

Figure 50

The chief use of double-faced fabrics is for blankets. Obviously, it is interesting to have a blanket with one color on one side and a contrasting one on the other, but aside from the appearance, this is a very useful weave. It really amounts to two fabrics being woven on a single warp, and since it is not the wool itself that is warm, but the air spaces between the fibers that make the insulation, a double fabric is more effective than a single one of equal weight. A blanket should not be woven hard and tight but should be loose and fluffy. Woolen yarn is better than worsted for the weft because it can be napped more easily.

PROBLEMS

1. Thread a loom with twill samples as shown in Fig. 51. With a standard tie-up weave as drawn in. A #5 perle cotton at 20 per inch and woven with a contrasting color shows up well.

2. Make a sample blanket on the draft at Fig. 51 by using the standard tie-up and at least 10 variations in treadling.

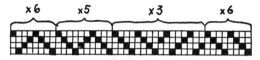

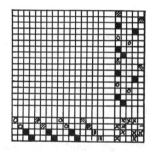

Figure 51

3. Make a sample blanket of at least 10 different patterns by using irregular tie-ups.
4. Repeat the treadling of Fig. 52 three times and work out the diagram analysis in three colors.

Figure 52

5. Make 25 designs on rosepath draft. Both standard and irregular tie-ups may be used. Colored pencils for color designs are suggested.

CHAPTER 5

Theory of Blocks

Since all weaving is accomplished by the interplay of warp and weft, all woven patterns as well as all structures are built on the basis of a square. This is plainly shown in the taffeta weave. If the warp and weft are of equal size and the cloth is perfectly balanced, both warp and weft are of equal value and the diagram is made as shown at Fig. 1. If the warp is very fine and is sleyed close together, and if the weft is a coarse yarn, the resulting fabric is called rep, faille, and so forth. If the weft is fine and is closely packed over a heavy warp, the resulting cloth has a tapestry effect. These three types of fabric are shown diagrammatically at Fig. 53. In actual cloth, neither the warp nor the weft squares need necessarily be square, but may be rectangles—their shape and size depending on the relative size of warp and weft.

In all weaving this principle of rectangles remains true. In brocades and damasks a line may appear to be curved, but if examined closely it will show a series of steps. The finer the thread and the closer the sley, the smaller will be the squares, rectangles and steps, and consequently the more flowing and curved the line will appear. At Fig. 54 two circles were drawn

Figure 53

having the same diameter. At A the circle was drawn on squared paper having just half as many squares per inch as the paper on which B was drawn. In both cases, the steps followed as closely as possible the curved line of the circle. While A passes for a circle, B is more obviously one, but the steps are still apparent. This principle of squares and rectangles holds just as true of design and pattern as it does of weave and texture.

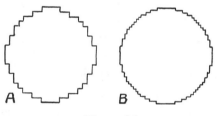

Figure 54

In making designs for handloom weaving then, the first thing is to know this theory of *block* designs, for by means of it almost any weave may be fitted to a given pattern. This chapter will deal exclusive with *pattern* as distinct from texture or structure or any method or type of weave. It is purely abstract and has nothing to do with the loom. Polka dot is a kind of pattern—it may be printed on voile, on taffeta, on satin, on percale, or on any other kind of fabric. There may be large dots or small ones, regularly or irregularly spaced. The pattern still remains a pattern entirely apart from the fabric on which it is used. Similarly in handweaving there are all kinds of patterns—star, circle, table, and so on. All patterns may be used for two or more types of fabric, though some patterns are more suitable for one type than another; for instance, a pattern that is good for summer-and-winter might very well be utterly unsuitable for M's and O's. In this chapter, pattern is pattern only and has nothing to do with any kind of weave; and the designs are not meant to be woven. They are made to show the principles of design as they apply to weaving.

TWO-BLOCK PATTERNS

The diagram of a taffeta weave looks like a checkerboard: there are two and only two sets of squares or rectangles. The simplest pattern, like the simplest weave, is the two-block pattern.

In any successful design the background plays an important part and should be as interesting as the pattern—in fact, it should be as much a part of the pattern as the more prominent element of the pattern itself. In weaving designs we must, to a certain extent, ignore the background, for in fitting the draft to the pattern, the black blocks only are considered; and this is true because of the mechanics of the loom. If the draft is written correctly for the pattern blocks, however, the background will take care of itself.

In twills and texture weaves it is the interplay of single warp and single weft threads that makes the texture or design. In pattern weaves it is the interplay of *groups* of warp threads and *groups* of weft threads that makes the design.

Fig. 55 shows the simplest pattern, the black blocks making the design. At the lower right-hand corner, the first square is black and can be called the A block. (Blocks are named by letters so that there will be no confusion with the numbered harnesses.) The warp threads which make that A block (or any other block) do not change their position during the whole process of weaving any given piece of cloth. Therefore, the whole vertical column belongs to Block A, literally from bottom to top. Any black rectangle in this column is an A block. And horizontally, the same is true. The weft threads pass from one selvage to the other of the cloth and there are as many picks

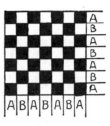

Figure 55

on the right edge as on the left edge. The first horizontal space belongs to Block A. Just as in cloth diagrams, so in pattern diagrams, where the A weft crosses the A warp, a pattern block (represented by a black square) results. The facts lead to the following rules.

Rule 1. ALL PATTERN BLOCKS IN ANY GIVEN VERTICAL ROW ARE THE SAME WIDTH AND ALL PATTERN BLOCKS IN ANY GIVEN HORIZONTAL ROW ARE THE SAME HEIGHT.

The second space to the left in the first horizontal row is white, but in the second horizontal row, as well as in the second vertical row, the square is black. This then is not an A block but an entirely new block, which can be called Block B. It conforms to Rule 1, just as the A block did. In placing Block B, we find

Rule 2. PATTERN BLOCKS PROGRESS IN A DIAGONAL DIRECTION.

The third space, whether diagonal, vertical, or horizontal, is black. It was established by Rule 1 that all black squares in the first vertical row as well as in the first horizontal row belong to Block A. The third space, therefore, is an A block. Where the A weft (horizontal) crosses the A warp (vertical) the resulting space is an A block. The diagonal third square is also an A square. Whether this design is read horizontally or vertically, every space is either an A or a B block. Only two blocks make this pattern—Block A and Block B.

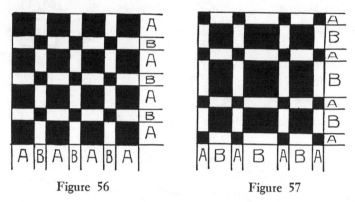

Figure 56   Figure 57

In Fig. 56 all the A blocks have been made twice their original width and height while the B blocks remain unchanged. In Fig. 57 the A blocks are represented in their original size while two of the B blocks have been made twice their original width and height and the third B block has been made three times its original size. This illustrates

Rule 3. ANY OR ALL BLOCKS IN A PATTERN MAY VARY IN HEIGHT OR WIDTH OR BOTH.

In the making of two-block patterns, the most important factor perhaps is variation in size. The two blocks are definitely placed and no rearrangement is possible, but any amount of variation in size is permissible so long as it improves the design.

Monk's Belt is an excellent example of good design in two-block pattern. The repetition in a single unit has a definite and pleasing rhythm, and the units themselves repeat smoothly. The individual rectangles are for the most part in the ratio of one to three, and the groups are in the ratio of three to five. It is a simple design but it has a definite center of interest—the eye always returns to the main unit. There is also a secondary or balancing unit (Fig. 58).

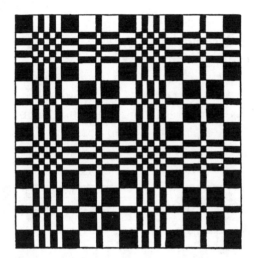

Figure 58

Charles A. Holmes

Figure 59

Another excellent two-block design is shown at Fig. 59. It has more variety and perhaps a better balance.

THREE-BLOCK PATTERNS

Fig. 60 is the simplest three-block pattern possible. At the lower right corner, the first two blocks are identical with A and B of the two-block pattern, and are easily recognized as A and B in this, a three-block pattern. The third space is neither A nor B, and according to Rule 2 is a new block entirely, Block C. If A, B, and C are repeated as A and B were in Fig. 55, a diagonal pattern, not a checkerboard, results.

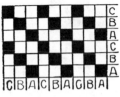

Figure 60

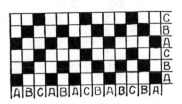

Figure 61

In Fig. 61 the vertical spaces are lettered (beginning at the right) A, B, C, B, A, C, B, A, B, C, B, A; and the horizontal spaces are lettered A, B, C, A, B, C. The diagram is plotted exactly as a cloth diagram is plotted. Where the horizontal A crosses the vertical A, a black rectangle results; similarly, where B crosses B and where C crosses C. The resulting pattern is reminiscent of a point twill and, as with a point twill, we find

Rule 4. THE DIRECTION OF PROGRESSION MAY REVERSE ON ANY BLOCK.

At Fig. 62 the vertical as well as the horizontal rows have been reversed in direction with a resulting diamond or diaper pattern. The guide lines in this diagram have been omitted and, unless the blocks are counted, it might pass for a diagram of a part of the old Colonial pattern (four-block) known as Governor's Garden.

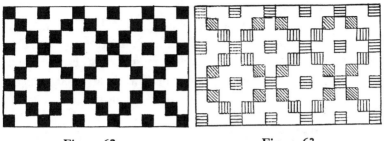

Figure 62   Figure 63

The same pattern is drawn at Fig. 63 but the blocks are identified by lines. All A blocks are drawn with horizontal lines, all B blocks with vertical lines, and all C blocks with diagonal lines. It is obvious in this drawing that all blocks stay within their own bounds (Rule 1). In the vertical A column there is always a pattern block where it is crossed by a horizontal A row. Never does a pattern block result by crossing the vertical A space by any other than a horizontal A space. And the same is true, of course, for the B spaces and for the C spaces. An A pattern block *must* result at every intersection of A vertical with A horizontal, but *only* where A crosses A. And the same is true of the B and C blocks. This is summed up in

Rule 5. A PATTERN BLOCK MUST RE-SULT AT EVERY INTERSECTION OF IDENTICALLY NAMED ROWS, BUT AT THE INTERSECTION OF IDENTICALLY NAMED ROWS ONLY.

At Fig. 64 is a three-block pattern in one repeat of which the blocks are identified by lines and in the remaining repeats by solid squares.

Figure 64

FOUR-BLOCK PATTERNS

With the rules for block patterns that have been established, four-block designing is a simple matter. It must be remembered that these rules are for *designs* only. Each type of weave has its own idiosyncracies which must be fitted into the design, or to which the design must be adjusted by minor changes.

To review the rules for block designs:

1. All pattern blocks in any vertical row are the same width and all pattern blocks in any horizontal row are the same height.
2. Pattern blocks progress in a diagonal direction.
3. Any or all blocks in a pattern may vary in height or width or both.
4. The direction of progression may reverse on any block.
5. A pattern block must result at every intersection of identically named horizontal and vertical rows, but at the intersection of identically named rows only.

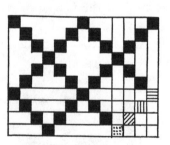

Figure 65

The simplest four-block pattern is a diamond, as shown at Fig. 65. All the blocks are the same size. Direction reverses at regular intervals. Compare this with Fig. 62 and note the difference that the fourth block makes.

It will be noticed that in all patterns so far shown, the blocks have followed a direct sequence: A, B, C, D, A, B, C, D. B is preceded by A or C and is followed by A or C. This cannot be called a rule for there are too many exceptions, particularly in patterns for summer-and-winter and in patterns of more than four blocks. Broken sequence is sometimes found in

Colonial overshot four-block patterns that are drafted on opposites. But there is then a

GUIDING PRINCIPLE: BLOCKS PROGRESS IN AN UN-
BROKEN SEQUENCE.

Any block may be designated as A; the one next to it will
be either B or D; but A must be consistently A throughout the
whole design, as must all other blocks be consistent.

It is not at all uncommon to find broken sequence in the
treadling of any pattern no matter what the technique nor how
many blocks there are. The threading, however, is usually,
though not always, in an unbroken sequence. Fig. 66 illustrates
this point; the threading is unbroken and reversing; the treadling
is broken, unbroken, and reversed.

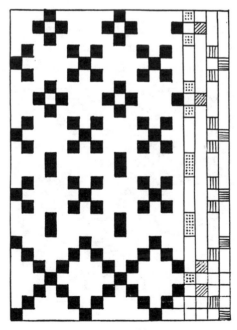

Figure 66

Identification of pattern by name is never very satisfactory, for the same patterns may be known by various names, often relating to different localities. Particularly is this true of the American Colonial patterns and of Swedish weaving. For instance, the familiar Colonial overshot weave is known in Sweden as "Daldräll" because it is extensively used in the province of Dalecarlia (Dalarne); "dräll" is the Swedish equivalent of twill. Often the name does not change, but because slight variations have occurred in the draft as it has passed from one weaver to another, several patterns exist with the same name. There are, however, general types of designs into which most patterns can be classified.

The simplest type of four-block pattern is the diamond; if woven with a broken sequence in the treadling, it becomes a cross pattern (Fig. 66). Usually in diamond patterns all blocks are the same size or nearly the same size. It is the uniformity of the blocks that gives the diamond or square shape.

Radiating patterns might almost be called diamond patterns in reverse; the center of interest in a radiating design

Figure 67

Figure 68

being the intersection of the cross boundaries of the diamond. Fig. 67 is the radiating pattern known most commonly as Star of Bethlehem. It is definitely a diamond pattern and though the largest blocks in the pattern are the boundaries of the diamond, they do not give a feeling of enclosure but one of expansion and radiation from the intersections of the small blocks. The figure of the star is more dominant than its enclosing square. The Bow Knot type of design is another radiating pattern; the four quarters of the diamond are so arranged that the intersection of the boundary lines is the center of interest.

A simple variation of the four-block pattern is the table design: two blocks alternate with each other to make larger blocks. Fig. 68 is a table design known as North Carolina Beauty.

The designs that appear to be most elaborate are the wheel patterns, but if they are studied for a moment, they lose most of their mystery and become table designs that have made very free use of Rule 3. Even a two-block pattern may have an appearance of roundness if the squares are varied enough. Fig. 69 shows the change from a table to a wheel pattern. The left side of the illustration is the same as Fig. 68. On the right side, the sizes of the blocks have been changed and a B block has added a star effect which makes the group of four small tables appear as four distinct units rather than as a large table.

Figure 69

Many designs combine two or more types of pattern to advantage. Double Chariot Wheel is a happy combination of wheels and tables. Governor's Garden combines diamonds and tables. Usually a table is used as a plain motif to separate and accent the more elaborate wheel or star pattern; it is a rest to the eye from the more confusing parts of the whole. Especially is the table a soothing influence when used with confusing radiating patterns such as Blooming Flower and Bow Knot. In the making of designs, this balancing of interest should be remembered. Two elaborate patterns combined will be confusing and disturbing (even one elaborate pattern is often disturbing!) and two plain patterns will tend to be monotonous and uninteresting. When units are combined, they should be such as harmonize with and complement each other.

FIVE-BLOCK PATTERNS

Five-block patterns and those having more than five blocks follow the same rules as other patterns. With more blocks, it is sometimes easier to obtain desired results, and more freedom is possible in arrangement. Even so, they must follow the limitations of two-, three- and four-block patterns as outlined in the five rules and one guiding principle of this chapter. These patterns will be discussed more fully in the chapters dealing with the various weaves and techniques.

ORIGINAL DESIGNS

After becoming familiar with the various types of designs and the qualifications of good design, one finds it an easy step to make original designs for weaving. Graph paper is essential. Colored pencils are a help also, for a different color may be assigned to each block; for instance, the A block may always be drawn with green, the B with orange, the C with violet and the D with blue. Any set of colors may be used, but they should be of nearly equal value so that the design as a whole will not have a distorted appearance. If colored pencils are used, it is easy to detect a mistake at a glance, and the offending block may be moved easily to its proper row without the necessity of counting and checking from the beginning square. Figs. 63 to 66, 68 and 69 have lines instead of color to designate the different blocks. A horizontal line block never appears in a row belonging to a vertical line block. With color it is easy to see that a green block is never placed in a row belonging to a blue block. For permanent records ink may be used; it has the advantage of not smudging as crayon does. But for working, colored pencil that may be erased if necessary is much better.

Whether one works from the whole to the parts or from the parts to the whole in making a design is a matter of individual preference. Probably the former is more direct and time saving, for it may eliminate later adjustment to size of yarn and reed and there is less of the trial-and-error method involved.

TO MAKE A DESIGN

The first thing is to discard timidity. Start with pencil and eraser and plenty of squared paper. In buying the paper don't try to be too economical. The first attempt may not be good, and even the tenth may not be too much better, but every design attempted means something learned. Four-block design-making can be more fascinating than working crossword puzzles, and to handweavers it is a more profitable way of spending time.

An easy beginning is a table design. The first thing to do is to break up the whole unit into interesting proportions and to line it off into rows, as shown at Fig. 70. To avoid confusion in black and white illustrations, the drawings following Fig. 70 have been ruled on plain paper rather than on squared paper. The proportions have been kept identical.

Table designs are made by alternating any two blocks with each other and then alternating the other two blocks. Beginning at the lower right-hand corner of Fig. 70, the rows are called A, B, A, B, A. Fig. 70 is a bi-symmetrical arrangement of lines and spaces; so the five rows on the extreme left are named A, B, A, B, A also. Since D is usually next to A, the center spaces are named D, C,

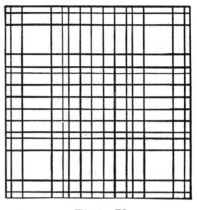

Figure 70

D, C, D. The horizontal spaces are named in the same order as the vertical ones. A design need not have the same order in horizontal as in vertical rows, but if a pattern is made this way, that is, to be woven as drawn in, a general idea of the pattern as a whole is formed, and changes in treadling (horizontal rows) suggest themselves more readily. In the first horizontal row, all

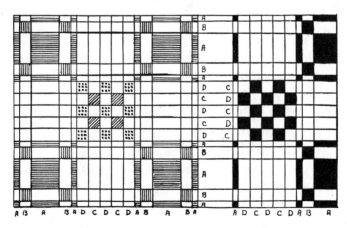

Figure 71

A blocks are filled in with green pencil or lines, according to Rule 5. Progressing upward in the same way, all B blocks are filled in with orange pencil or vertical lines; all C blocks with violet pencil or diagonal lines, and all D blocks with blue pencil or dots. As soon as the whole design is filled in, a rearrangement of the treadling order of the C and D blocks suggests itself to avoid the checkerboard effect of the center table. The horizontal rows are transposed to read C, D, C, D, C, as shown in the black portion of Fig. 71. This second arrangement of the center table is, according to some weavers, woven "rose fashion" rather than "star fashion."

The same set of lines (Fig. 70) might be used for a diamond pattern and a different method of design used. The center group of squares, five wide and five high, immediately suggests a diamond. A three-block diamond is drawn as shown at Fig. 72. It is drawn in before designating any row as belonging to any block. The diamond is to be the basis for further development of the design. With the diamond established, the next step is to identify the blocks and rows.

The black square at the bottom of the diamond and in the center vertical row makes a logical beginning. It is named Block A. Therefore, "A" is written below this square at the bottom of the diagram and in its proper place in the horizontal space. It is now clear that this design is not to be woven as drawn in, for the vertical and horizontal rows belonging to the A block are not in identical positions. The blocks on either side of A will be either B or D. For convenience, these are named B, and the two B's are written in place for the vertical and horizontal rows. According to Rule 2, the two remaining black squares are C blocks. Two C's are written for the two vertical rows, and a C for the horizontal row.

In accordance with the Guiding Principle, and because this is to be a diamond type of design, the small rows adjacent to the vertical C's and the horizontal A's are named "D." The D squares are filled in with their proper color or symbol.

Next to the two small vertical rows (D rows) must be either A or C. If C is chosen, making the small D a reversing point, another diamond will result, but it will be distorted in shape because all the blocks are not square, nor of the same size. Instead of reversing at D, the next two blocks progress in a continuous direction from the center. They are named A and B and are so designated at the bottom of the diagram on both sides of the center group. The horizontal rows are not named for the time being. With the exception of the two outside rows on each side, the vertical rows have been assigned and read B, A, D, C, B, A (center), B, C, D, A, B. The seven horizontal rows in the center have been assigned and read D, A, B, C (center), B, A, D. With this many rows known, as many blocks as possible are filled in with their proper colors or symbols. At this point of development, the design looks like Fig. 72.

With this much done, the design has really made itself. The D, A, and B blocks at each side of the original diamond

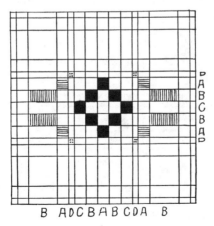

Figure 72

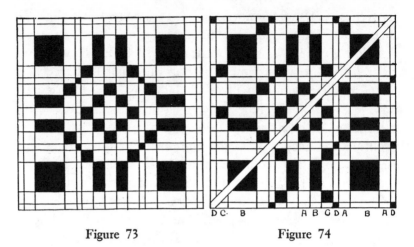

Figure 73   Figure 74

immediately suggest themselves for the top and bottom parts of the design. Following this natural tendency of the design, the large squares at the corners automatically become B blocks and the only remaining problem is what to do with the two outside rows of the pattern (Fig. 73).

Two possibilities suggest themselves; they are shown at Fig. 74 on opposite sides of the diagonal dividing line. At the

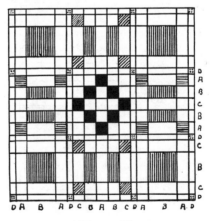

Figure 75

lower right triangle the large B space has been used as a reversing point making the space next to it A and the small edge
space D. At the upper left triangle, the sequence continues in
the same direction; thus the space next to the large B becomes
C and the outside space D. The design as planned in the lower
right side of the diagonal is completed in its proper symbols
at Fig. 75.

Figure 76

All designs will not repeat equally well. Two straight-edged mirrors are most convenient tools in designing. They may be moved along different lines and by reflecting parts of the design show quickly the most advantageous lines and spaces to use for reversing points. Held at right angles, two mirrors will give complete repeats of design in both directions.

When a unit of design is completed, it should always be repeated on graph paper at least twice in each direction and studied carefully to determine what changes, if any, should be made in proportion and arrangement.

Fig. 76 shows some of the designs just completed when drawn out in repeats. At the top, the table design of Fig. 71 makes a successful surface pattern. At the lower left, Fig. 75 has been repeated. The large squares are rather overpowering and the tiny D block in the center seems entirely lost; this design clearly needs more work. At the lower right, the large blocks have been eliminated entirely with an unbalanced effect.

Fig. 77 is a composite. Several designs were made, none of which was entirely good, but each had possibilities. The good points were collected and the bad ones eliminated; the original proportions are completely lost, but the design as a whole has benefited.

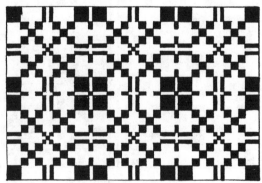

Figure 77

Wheel or circle patterns may be made in various ways. One method, already described, is that of changing the proportion of a table design. Other methods are illustrated at Figs. 78 and 79.

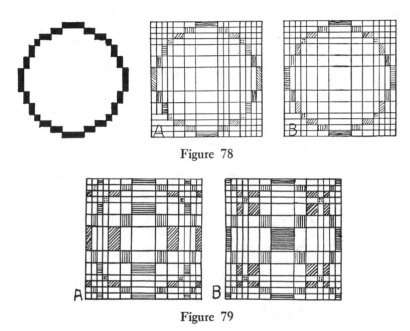

Figure 78

Figure 79

At Fig. 54A a circle was traced following as nearly as possible the lines of the cross-section paper. At Fig. 78 this same circle is used, but instead of a single line describing the circle, the entire squares have been filled in so as to make the *blocks* describe the circle. At A of Fig. 78 the blocks have been filled in symbolically to designate them as A, B, C and D. Horizontal and vertical lines have been drawn to complete the square and to make the guide lines for all blocks. At A of Fig. 79, all blocks have been filled in to complete the design.

At B of Fig. 78, the same outline of blocks has been used but the blocks have been named differently. The beginning has been made at the four long narrow blocks at top, bottom, and both sides; all are named "A." The two blocks on each side of the A blocks are named "B"; the next adjacent blocks are named "C" and the remaining little blocks automatically become "D." All circles will not work by this method of designating. In this particular circle there are an odd number of blocks between the starting points. Had there been an even number, that is, had there been no little square to become the D block, two C blocks would have come next to each other, an arrangement which of course would not have worked. At B of Fig. 79 all blocks have been filled in to complete the design.

Figure 80

Figure 81

At Fig. 80 the design in Fig. 79A has been repeated to show its "all-over" effect and has been elaborated with *very* poor results. This illustrates again that the simpler designs are usually the best. A circle in itself is elaborate enough and it cannot well stand decoration. Fig. 81 is somewhat better, for here the circles have been subordinated to the whole and there is not so much confusion.

In Fig. 82 a larger circle has been used as a beginning with rather unusual results. The blocks have been named beginning at all four points; had they been named by beginning in the center and working outward in a continuous progression, the side blocks would still have been the same as the beginning ones with a resulting large square in the center, and instead of a cross through the middle of the design, there would have been a large block in the exact center and an inner concentric circle.

Amelia D. White

Figure 82

Fig. 83 shows the results of an interesting experiment. The outline of Fig. 70 was sent to six different persons who were asked to make designs from it. No restrictions were imposed— the design could be for any weave and for any number of blocks. This was strictly a problem in design. Five of the six responded and sent in twenty-eight designs. The most amazing feature of the experiment was that there was no duplication. Surely this is proof positive that there is still much new to be found in the field of weaving patterns.

A design may be analyzed just as a weave may be. It will have a pattern diagram, a pattern draft for threading (also called a profile or a short draft), a pattern draft for treadling, and a pattern draft for tie-up. *The pattern draft for threading must not be confused with the eventual threading draft. The pattern draft applies to blocks only and the threading draft is derived from it after the type of weave is determined.*

Fig. 84 is a simple illustration of a pattern analysis. There is nothing about it to suggest what kind of cloth it might be;

Charles A. Holmes   Amelia D. White

Isobel Brazelton   Clarice Butcher

Figure 83

in fact, it is hard to imagine why it should ever have been woven in any kind of cloth! But it does tell us several things. In the first place, it shows what the pattern is. Secondly, it

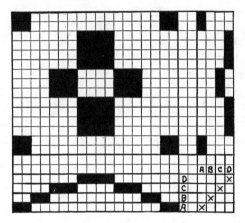

Figure 84

indicates a four-block pattern and that when making the pattern draft for it, we must write two units of Block A, two units of Block B, three of C, four of D, three of C, two of B, and finally two units of A. Thirdly, the pattern tie-up tells us that each block is woven alone; no two blocks are combined. And in the fourth place, the pattern draft for treadling tells us that in order to weave the pattern as shown, we will treadle two units of A, then four units of D, three of C, four of D, and, to finish, two of A. The B block has not been used in the treadling.

PROBLEMS
1. Identify as A, B, C, and D the blocks of several known weaving patterns.
2. Make a two-block pattern suitable for a baby blanket 40 x 72 inches.
3. Make a three-block pattern for a linen towel. Blocks may vary in size, but there should not be too great a difference in size; they may be kept in the proportion of 1, 1½ and 2 squares on the cross-section paper.
4. Expand a four-block diamond pattern to a radiating pattern.
5. Make a four-block table pattern and adjust it to a wheel pattern.

6. Make as many designs as possible using the rulings as shown in Fig. 85.

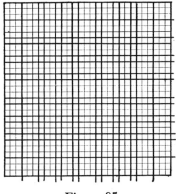

Figure 85

7. Make at least two designs using Fig. 86 as a basis.

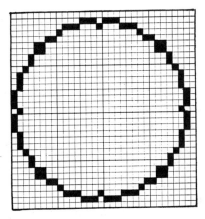

Figure 86

CHAPTER 6

M's and O's

Having learned to make patterns, regardless of how they are to be woven, you are now ready to apply the structure to the pattern.

Handwoven fabrics can be divided into definite groups, each separate from the others and each having special characteristics which make it unmistakably distinguishable from all others.

In a department store there is no possibility of confusing taffeta with satin or velvet with serge. Each of these fabrics has its own characteristic structure regardless of color, fiber or, possibly, pattern. So it is with handwoven fabrics. Tabby and twill as we have seen have their own structures but their variations in appearance are due chiefly to the yarns and the color arrangements used. With other handwoven fabrics, the structure makes the pattern and distinguishes each fabric, one from the other. We are now ready to discuss these more intricate fabrics.

M's and O's is actually a form of twill, but because it is so often woven in a pattern and because of its many variations, it is deserving of a classification of its own and its own chapter.

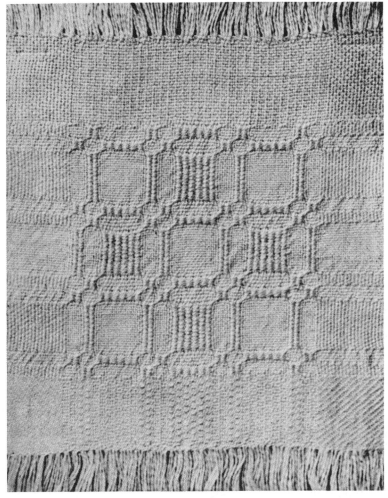

Figure 87

What connection there is between this useful weave and the two letters of the alphabet seems to be one of the deep dark secrets of the past. While the weave was extensively used in Colonial times, the name has not been definitely connected with it till more recent years. This weave is found in many lands and is used for many purposes. In the Scandinavian countries it is woven with heavy yarns for upholstery materials as well as with finer yarns for curtains. Hulda Peters in her *Vävbok* gives one tablecloth draft in this weave, but calls it "fattigmansdräll." The usual fattigmansdräll, or "poor man's damask," is quite a different type of weaving, more like a modified "daldräll" or Colonial overshot. In the *Vävboken* of Montell-Glantzberg, M's and O's is called "halvdräll," or half-twill. Most Scandinavian writers call this weave simply "jump twill" and in America it is widely known as "linen weave." Fig. 87 shows a small sampler of M's and O's. When it is examined, it is seen to have certain characteristics that make it easily distinguishable from other fabrics.

Apparent characteristics. M's and O's is a two-thread construction; that is, it is woven with only one shuttle and on a single warp. Depending on how it is treadled, it may be a texture weave rather than a pattern weave, but the texture may be enlarged to make a very definite two-block pattern. The pattern blocks are formed by small alternating overshots of weft which enclose groups of warp threads to form a corded effect. There are at least two heavy cords in each block of pattern and usually there is an even number of cords. The area that is not corded pattern block is tabby background and the two blocks are interchangeable; that is, what is pattern in one row of design becomes tabby in the following row, and the tabby becomes pattern.

The fabric is identical on both sides, both in pattern and structure. This is the distinguishing characteristic of M's and O's. No other fabric is identical in pattern as well as structure on both sides of the piece.

Structural characteristics. All of the apparent characteristics are structural, for it is the structure that makes the appearance of the fabric. But in looking at a piece of M's and O's, one does not always see that there is no true tabby possible from selvage to selvage. And although it is a form of twill, there is also no true twill from edge to edge.

Design. In Chapter 5, designs were made without regard to the type of fabric. To be successfully woven, however, a design must be made for the type of fabric in which it is to be produced as well as for the ultimate use to which that fabric is to

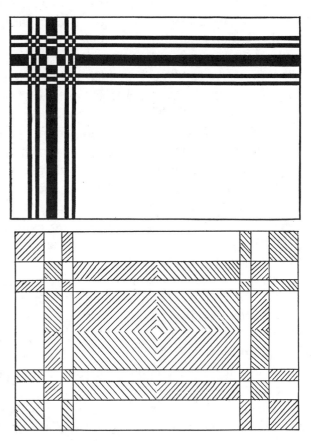

Figure 88

84   DESIGNING AND DRAFTING FOR HANDWEAVERS

be put, and consideration must also be given to the yarn to be used. M's and O's is good for an all-over or repeat design for upholstery (Fig. 94) or a unit design to fit an individual piece, such as a place mat, baby blanket, or stole (Fig. 88). Usually the large blocks should be the tabby blocks, for the pattern blocks are less firm in construction and unless there are equally large tabby blocks to surround them, the pattern blocks have a tendency to pull out of shape. In making the design, one must bear in mind that a single unit of pattern consists of *two* vertical cords. Usually a block consists of an even number of cords, but this is not compulsory. A single cord or half unit can be made in the draft, though it is rarely satisfactory.

Draft writing. As stated above, M's and O's is a twill adaptation. Block A is drafted 1-2-3-4, a direct twill. Block B is drafted 1-3-2-4 (Fig. 89). This is, of course, the simplest possible form. Each unit of the design is divided into two parts so that each unit makes two of the heavy cords in the pattern block. In Block A, 1—2 constitutes one half of the unit and 3—4 the second half. In Block B, 1—3 makes one half of the unit and 2—4 makes the second half. This means that in the woven cloth, there are two ends in each group of warps forming the cords of the blocks. Naturally, this means a small pattern, in fact so small that it is hardly a pattern at all but merely a texture.

Figure 89

In most pattern drafting, a unit of design consists of a fixed number of warp-ends and a block is enlarged by repeating that unit as often as desired. In M's and O's the unit may be enlarged as well as repeated. The unit is expanded by repeating each half of it.

In Fig. 90 the units have been enlarged. At X there are three warp-ends in each group, making six ends in a unit. For the most part, when M's and O's is considered as a pattern

weave, there are eight ends in each unit as at Y of Fig. 90. If
the fabric is sleyed at 15 ends per inch, this will mean that the
overshots are approximately one-quarter inch wide, which is
about the limit for good weaving. If a very fine warp is used
and quite closely sleyed, the unit can be expanded to 12 ends
with six ends in each group as at Z of Fig. 90.

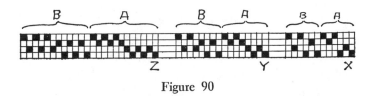

Figure 90

The pattern analysis of the center only of the sampler
shown at Fig. 87 is given at Fig. 91. It is a pattern diagram with
pattern drafts. To write the threading draft is a simple matter.
The eight-end unit is used. The first unit of the design is a B
block. At Fig. 92 one unit of the formula for the B block is
written first. There is a single unit of A and the eight ends of
the A unit are added next. The third block of the pattern is a
three-unit B block and it is written next. To shorten the draft,

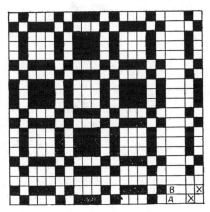

Figure 91

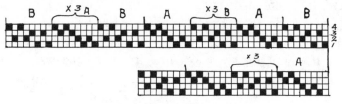

Figure 92

a bracket is drawn above the group, with "X 3" above it to indicate that the B group is used three times. This method is continued until all the blocks in the pattern draft have been translated to a threading draft.

When one writes the threading draft for any pattern, it is important to give the unit the proper number of warp-ends. This will depend upon the size of the warp and upon how closely it is to be set in the reed. Naturally a large number of warp-ends in a group makes for loose weaving in that block, and since the adjacent block is a tabby weave, the weft will not pack closely in the pattern blocks. When the units are too large the resulting cloth is likely to be sleazy and shapeless.

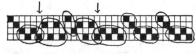

Figure 93

All half-units, or cords, of the block need not be the same size, but for a balanced effect in the block, there must be an extra half-unit, making an odd number of cords. This will prevent a clean-cut line between the blocks, for it is impossible in the draft to avoid having one warp thread that is common to both blocks in the pattern (Fig. 93). In the woven cloth this makes a break in the rhythm and looks like a mistake. If every block has an extra half-unit, so that there is a common warp thread between all blocks, the "mistake" is not so obvious. If this "mistake" is very carefully handled, it may on some occasions add to the interest of the pattern. In an all-over pattern, however, if all the blocks have varied sizes of units, there is no gain in interest, but rather an increase in confusion. Generally it is better to keep to the regular formula of the draft. In a design such as the top one of Fig. 88, the size of units may be varied safely and quite interestingly; the larger blocks should have the smaller units.

The direction of the twill, whether right or left, is immaterial, but the same direction must always be kept in any single draft. One look at a draft will show the importance of keeping the direction constant. Each unit and each half-unit must be kept a separate entity. If the direction changes and the twill becomes a point twill, it is obvious that the "mistake" of a common warp-end in adjacent blocks will be repeated many times and the cords will lose all identity. The weaving is no longer M's and O's nor can it be called a successful example of that heterogeneous classification known as "novelty weave."

Tie-up. When looking at a threading draft to find the tie-up, one usually tries to find first that combination of harnesses which will pick up alternate threads of the warp to produce tabby. On a draft for M's and O's it is impossible to find any combination of harnesses which will produce alternate ends. Therefore, on M's and O's there is no true tabby possible.

Block A is drafted by using 1—2 as one half of the unit and its opposite, 3—4, as the second half of the unit. Therefore, the combination of harnesses 1 and 2 will produce an overshot to make part of the pattern as will the combination of harnesses 3 and 4. Block B is drafted by using 1—3 and its opposite 2—4 for the two halves of its unit, and so the combinations of 1—3 and 2—4 become the pattern combinations to weave the B block. Of the six possible combinations of two harnesses on a four-harness loom, four combinations are needed to weave the pattern. The two remaining combinations of 1—4 and 2—3 produce neither tabby nor pattern. The tie-up for M's and O's is the standard tie-up, but in weaving a pattern, only four of the six combinations are used.

Treadling. Fig. 94 shows a photograph of a material used for drapery. It is woven from fine silk, several strands of which were used together as a single yarn. The draft and diagram of the cloth are given at Fig. 95. Block A is threaded 1-2-1-2-3-4-3-4. The tie-up indicates that if the combinations of 1—2 and 3—4 are treadled alternately, Block A will result. Similarly, the combinations 1—3 and 2—4, if treadled alternately, will produce Block B. In looking at Fig. 94 and Fig. 95 one sees that this fabric is woven as drawn in. The fabric as well as the diagram shows plain tabby blocks alternating with pattern blocks; the pattern blocks are formed by short weft skips enclosing groups of warp threads. To produce a firmer cloth, the largest blocks of the pattern were woven in tabby.

Variations in weave or texture help to make M's and O's the interesting fabric that it is. With only four of the six combinations of the standard tie-up used to produce the pattern, the question naturally arises: "If 1—4 and 2—3 combinations produce neither pattern nor tabby, what *do* they produce?" The answer is interesting. If there are four ends in each unit of design, the blocks of the pattern disappear entirely, and the resulting fabric becomes a weft-faced rep. If the eight-end unit is used, the result is more interesting. Again the blocks of the pattern disappear but in the resulting fabric every third warp appears to be twice the size of the others. If the twelve-end unit is used, every fifth warp will look heavy (Fig. 96A).

With any fabric that calls for the standard tie-up, the use of a twill treadling is natural. In M's and O's if the four-end unit is treadled in a direct twill, the resulting fabric is sure to have an interesting texture. The effect is of alternating twill

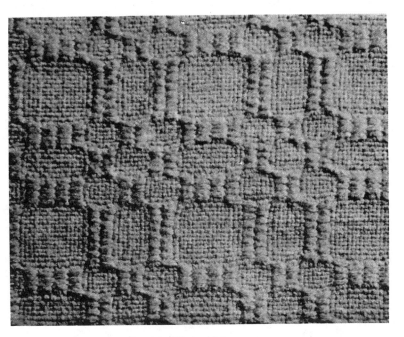

Figure 94

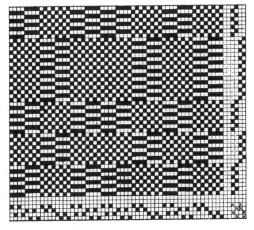

Figure 95

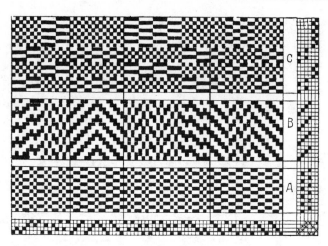

Figure 96

and granite. If the direct twill is repeated twice and the broken twill is repeated three or four times, the result is an interesting variation of a tweed for wearing apparel.

When the eight-thread units are used, the twill stripe is more interesting than the serge one. If the stripes are well-proportioned, M's and O's woven with a twill treadling makes a beautiful fabric. The direction of the twill makes little, if any, difference in effect (Fig. 96B).

Fig. 96 is a small sampler of M's and O's showing possible variations in both threading and treadling. In the threading draft, the direction of the direct twill has been reversed to make a point twill, but the broken twill which immediately follows has also changed its direction. Thus the relation of broken twill to direct twill remain constant.

At C of Fig. 96 is shown the diagram of the fabric when woven for pattern. Some of the units are small and some are larger eight-end units. Enlarging the treadling draft does not change the texture in any way—it merely changes the size of the pattern blocks.

A little study of the sampler (Fig. 96) shows three separate and distinct fabrics: near-tabby, near-twill, and pattern. The pattern is still further varied by the effects of the small units and the larger ones. Because of these definite differences, the use of all variations in any one piece of weaving will produce very definite horizontal stripes, for the fabrics do not mix. It is difficult to achieve a well-balanced design combining all three types of treadling or threading, but two variations will often combine with excellent results.

Fig. 97 is a diagram of a fabric in which pattern and twill are happily combined. The draft for this pattern (Fig. 98) is interesting because it is one of the few cases in which it is possible to mix the directions of the twills. The broken twill at the beginning of the repeat is a twill to the left, while the repeat ends with a twill to the right. When this warp is threaded, at one of the junctions of the wide stripe of twill with the stripe of broken twill there is a single warp-end that is going to be out-of-step no matter how the draft is written. But the pattern as a whole is large enough so that this apparent mistake is not too noticeable. The only way to avoid it would be to have one stripe of twill point up and the next point down; but this would destroy completely the unity of the design. There are five variations in texture, and to make a variation in pattern would result in confusion. Note that where this fabric is woven as a pattern, the large blocks are the small four-end units of the A block (the point twill) and the small blocks of either A or B are the eight-end units of pattern.

The small four-end units make good fabrics for wearing apparel and for baby blankets—there are no long overshots to catch and pull. Often in the eight-end forms of M's and O's, the pattern blocks will be open and sleazy. By using the four-end form, pattern can still be achieved by treadling the blocks for twill and the background for granite instead of tabby (Fig. 88).

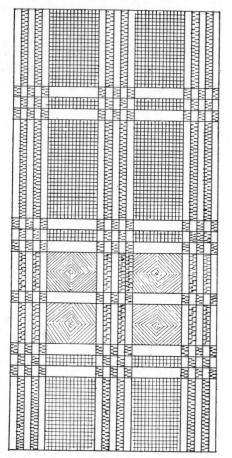

Figure 97

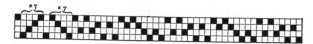

Figure 98

There are no problems in writing the threading draft; the only problem comes in the treadling. When changing from one block to the next, always start the new block on the opposite shed

from the last shot of the previous
block. The necessity for this is shown
in the change from the lower to the
middle block of Fig. 99. The change
from the middle block to the upper
block was done at random with the
result that there are long warp overshots—more than four warp on one
side of the fabric and more than
three on the reverse side. In the
actual fabric, this would be most unattractive.

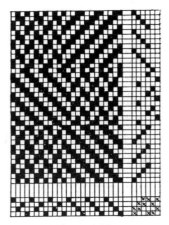

Figure 99

Usually M's and O's is a two-
block pattern, but it is perfectly
possible to use all three of the combinations of two harnesses.
The C block is then threaded 1-4-1-4-2-3-2-3 (Fig. 100). When
the A block is treadled, both the B and the C blocks automatically become tabby. When B is treadled, the A block is
tabby as usual, but in the C space the weave is not a true
tabby. When the C block is treadled for pattern, there is no
tabby background anywhere. If this problem is kept in mind
and the design is made accordingly, the irregularity of the
background can be made an asset rather than a liability.

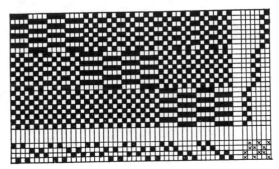

Figure 100

The success of M's and O's, perhaps more than that of any other fabric, is dependent on the yarns used. Generally speaking, a soft yarn which will pack well without making the resulting fabric stiff gives the best results. In linen, for instance, a single "flat" yarn will work better than a two-ply or three-ply "round" linen. Sley is equally important. The tabby portions should look like tabby and not like rep, but the weft must pack closely enough so that the pattern or corded portions are not sleazy. *Always* make samples to try out the yarn to be used; make several on various sized reeds to be sure that the proper balance is achieved.

PROBLEMS

1. Make a draft for the design at Fig. 87.
2. Make the treadling draft for Fig. 97.
3. Plan a tweed stripe arrangement and write the draft for it.
4. Write at least three threading drafts for each of the designs at Fig. 91.
5. On the loom, make a set of samples, using the draft at Fig. 101. Use several sizes of yarns, and weave each size on various sizes of reeds, and in various treadlings.

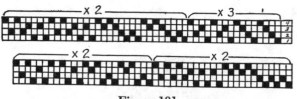

Figure 101

CHAPTER 7

Spot Bronson

"Spot bronson" is a name used today to designate a weave much used in Colonial times for linen, though in those days it was usually called "diaper." In 1817 J. and R. Bronson published their *Domestic Manufacturer's Assistant and Family Directory in the Arts of Weaving and Dyeing.* In their book they have given many drafts for "diaper," all written as we now write the drafts for so-called spot bronson. Most of the drafts are for looms of more than four harnesses (or, as the Bronsons called them, four-wing looms), a fact which seems to indicate that this weave was done more by the professional or village weaver on his multi-harness loom than by the home weaver.

In Scandinavian books the same weave is called "droppdräll" or "sjusprangdräll." In German books, it is called "Gerstenkornbindung" or "barleycorn." In old Colonial notebooks, it is often called merely "spot weave" or "speck weave." Actually, it is a form of huck—or possibly huck is a form of barleycorn! Huck has two spots in the pattern, whereas spot bronson (as it shall be called here) has three or more.

Apparent characteristics. Fig. 102 shows a small sample of spot bronson. It is a two-thread construction. There is only one

95

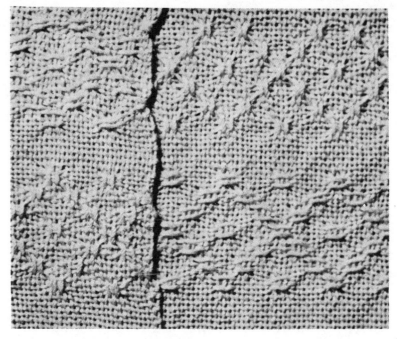

Figure 102

warp and it is woven with a single shuttle. The pattern is formed by small parallel overshots and the background is tabby. The blocks or spots may or may not vary in size. The pattern and background are interchangeable; what is pattern in one row becomes tabby in the next. The *pattern* is identical on both sides of the cloth. The distinguishing characteristic of this weave is that the overshots are warp on one side and weft on the other side. The bronson weaves are the only fabrics in which the pattern is identical on both sides, but with the overshots warp on one side and weft on the other. Whether the warp overshot or the weft overshot is considered the "right" side is a matter of personal preference. The ultimate use of the fabric will probably determine the choice.

Structural characteristics are, of course, the same as apparent characteristics, for it is the structure which makes the appearance. A further structural characteristic that is not visible in the woven cloth is the arrangement of the warp threads through the heddles (the threading draft) and the manner of treadling. One-half of all warp-ends, every alternate end, is on one harness and each remaining harness carries the warp threads for a single spot of pattern. Thus a three-block pattern is woven on a four-harness loom, a four-block pattern on a five-harness loom, and so on.

Design. Designs for spot bronson conform to all rules of block patterns generally. In a design for a four-harness loom, the

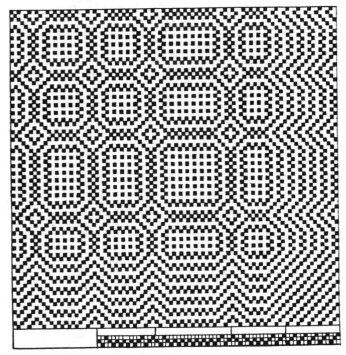

Figure 103

number of blocks must be kept to three. The blocks are usually small (hence the name spot) and when the size varies, the variation is not great. Fig. 103 shows the corner of a design for a towel in which the spots are all the same size. Fig. 104 is a design taken from an old tablecloth in which the sizes of the spots vary. The *pattern draft* for each design appears under the diagram. Fig. 103 is woven rose-fashion and Fig. 104 is woven star-fashion or as drawn in.

Figure 104

It is possible to combine blocks and to weave two at a time on a four-harness loom and two or more at a time on a multi-harness loom. The result of weaving two spots at a time on a four-harness loom is one larger spot, and this is seldom good. On a multi-harness loom, there is no problem.

Draft writing. When writing a draft for spot bronson, as for any other weave, one must first have a pattern draft. Every alternate thread is put on the #1 harness, which is the foundation harness. The warp threads for the A block are put on the #2 harness, the warps for the B block are on the #3 harness, and the warps for the C block are on the #4 harness. The same method is followed for as many blocks and harnesses as are called for in the design.

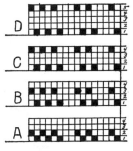

Figure 105

Generally there are four warp-ends to a unit, but in designs in which the sizes of the spots vary, the number of warp-ends will vary; there is, however, always an *even* number: two, four, six, and so on. The A spot is written 1-2-1-2 (or 2-1-2-1); the B is written 1-3-1-3; the C is written 1-4-1-4; the D is written 1-5-1-5, and so forth (Fig. 105).

The relation of pattern to pattern draft to threading draft is illustrated at Fig. 106. It shows a pattern diagram (not a cloth diagram) of a simple three-block or three-spot pattern that is not treadled as drawn in. The blocks comprising the pattern draft are under the pattern itself and are labeled A, B, and C. Below each pattern block is the threading draft for the warp-ends which make that block. In this design, since all spots are the same width, all have four ends.

The spots in bronson may vary in width, as determined by the number of warp-ends per spot. In the statement of characteristics, it was found that the spots are formed by weft overshots on one side of the cloth and warp overshots on the reverse side. If a fine warp is used and if it is closely spaced, the skips may be over more threads, but a skip of one-quarter inch or more is rarely practical or beautiful. In Fig. 104 some spots are three times and some are two times as large as the smallest spot. If four warp-ends are considered for the small spots, then the large spots will be twelve threads in width. With warps spaced at 30 or 32 ends per inch, the overshot will be almost half an inch, and much too long. In this pattern, then, it is better to use only two ends per unit, with six ends in the largest spot.

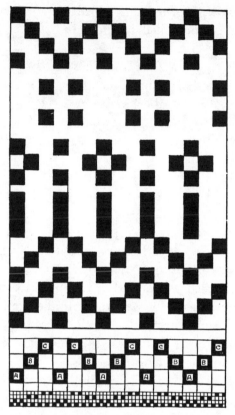

Figure 106

A satisfactory threading draft for Fig. 104 would probably be that at Fig. 107.

Combining spots. On a four-harness loom, with only three spots possible, it is not often that spots can be combined with any degree of success. With more harnesses, however, combinations can be made. If there are several spots in the design, and

Figure 107

if the combinations of spots are so arranged that no two adjacent spots are combined at any one time, no change need be made in the threading draft. At Fig. 108 are two designs made on the same six-spot pattern. No two adjacent blocks are used in any one row.

In Fig. 109, the same pattern draft has been used to make an entirely different pattern, even without the addition of the borders. In this pattern, adjacent (e and f) spots have been combined. If there are four warp-ends in each spot and five spots are combined, the resulting weft overshot will be more

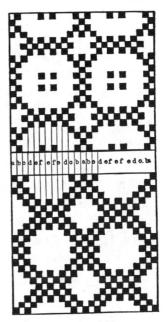

Figure 108

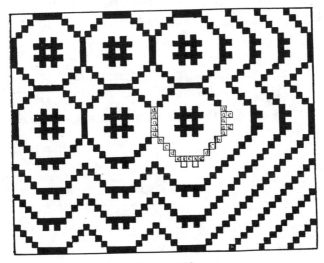

Figure 109

than 20 warp-ends, and this, of course, is unthinkable. Therefore, in the threading draft, a separating thread is added. This
will insure five spots in a row instead of a single spot of equal
width. The separating warps require a harness of their own
just as each spot requires its own harness. Therefore, while the
designs at Fig. 108 could be done on a seven-harness loom,
the design at Fig. 109 calls for eight harnesses.

The separating threads have another valuable use besides
eliminating the long overshot. By threading the separating
threads alternately with the foundation threads (in this case
1-8-1-8-1-8 etc.), one can make a plain tabby selvage. This is
a great help, for without the plain tabby a good edge on spot
bronson is most difficult. This grouping of tabby-weaving warps
may be introduced anywhere in the draft, so that there can be
longitudinal stripes of plain weave combined with stripes of
spot weave.

The separating threads may be placed on any single harness. It seems a bit more logical and perhaps less confusing to
place them on the back harness if the front one is used for the
foundation warps. Some weavers prefer putting them on the second harness, and this would not be in the least confusing if

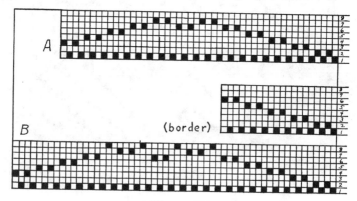

Figure 110

there were separating warps between all spots; but where there are only occasional separating warps, it seems a bit easier to put them on the back harness, regardless of its number.

The draft for Fig. 108 is given at A of Fig. 110 and for Fig. 109 at B.

Separating threads may be used between all spots if desired. In that case many more variations in treadling are possible, a distinct advantage in quantity production. When a separating thread is used, the spots do not meet so closely at the corners, and have a more scattered appearance. The woven pattern does not hold together, and in a pattern such as the one in Fig. 108 where the spots meet on the diagonal, the use of a separating thread is a distinct disadvantage.

To sum up the requirements of a spot bronson draft: alternate threads must be on a single harness; there are two threads or a multiple of two in each unit of the pattern; if adjacent spots are to be combined, there must be an extra harness to carry the separating warp-ends.

Tie-up. One look at a draft for spot bronson and the characteristic of alternate warps on a single harness is obvious. Since one-half of all the warps are alternately on one harness, this harness alone makes one of the tabby sheds. It takes *all* of the other harnesses, three or thirty, *used together* to make the second tabby shed.

Since the warp threads for Block A have been placed on harness 2, harnesses 1 and 2 will be combined to weave the A spot, 3 and 1 will weave the B spot, and 4 and 1 will weave the C spot. The pattern harness when used in combination with the foundation harness results in a spot when woven. This is true regardless of the number of harnesses used. If there are seven spots in the pattern, then the combination of harnesses 1 and 8 will be the combination needed to produce the G spot. If spots are combined, then the two or more pattern harnesses must be combined with the foundation harness. The only combination that is never used is the combination of the separating threads and the foundation threads.

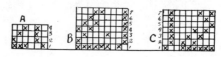

Figure 111

It will be seen from Fig. 111 that a simple tie-up for a three-spot, or four-harness bronson weave requires only five combinations, or five treadles. The tie-ups for Fig. 108 are given at B and C of Fig. 111. The tie-up for Fig. 109 is obvious. The order in which each combination is tied to its respective treadle is purely a matter of convenience to the individual weaver.

Weaving. Bronson is a two-thread construction. There is one warp and one weft—only one shuttle is used. It is a very speedy weave, if the loom gives a clear shed (a counterbalanced loom may not always do so).

The order of treadling follows exactly the order of threading. Use of the pattern combination forms the pattern, or design, of the fabric, and the use of the multiple-harness tabby combination forms the foundation of the fabric. This is more clearly shown in the diagram of the cloth at Fig. 112 than by any number of words.

In the weaving, if the single-harness tabby is on the left and the multiple harness is on the right, the direction of the shuttle will always follow the use of the tabby treadles. For plain weaving lower the single tabby harness and enter the shuttle from the left; next, lower the multiple-harness tabby and enter the shutter from the right. An invariable rule can be made: whenever the shuttle is to be entered from the right, *always* use a multiple-harness tabby. This rule never varies. When the shuttle is to be entered from the left, the pick may

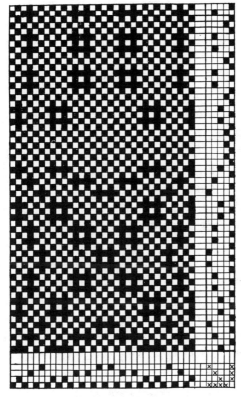

Figure 112

be either a tabby on the single harness or a pattern combination. If it is desired to elongate the pattern so that the spots do not meet exactly at the corners, or if the same spot is to be repeated in the length of the fabric, a single-harness tabby must be introduced between the spots. This does not change the treadling rule. Always and forever, with no exception, every alternate weft thread must be a multiple-harness tabby (see the top portion of Fig. 112).

Rising and falling sheds. The pattern in bronson, as in all other weaves, is affected by the mechanics of the loom. The fabric itself will be the same whether woven on a loom with a rising shed or one with a falling shed, both using the same tie-up. What happens in a bronson weave is that with a falling shed and the draft as given at Fig. 112, the side of the fabric having the weft overshots is the visible side when on the loom. The same draft when used on a loom with a rising shed will produce the identical fabric, but the warp overshots will be visible during the weaving.

Since it is more convenient to count the weft skips when they are easily visible, it is an advantage to have them on the top of the web. This can be accomplished on a rising-shed loom by transposing the harness combinations to the opposite ones. That is, instead of using the 1—4 combination, use the 2—3; instead of 1—3, use 2—4, and so forth. When the pattern combinations are transposed, it is most important to change the tabby combination also. When weaving with a rising shed, it is the single-harness tabby that follows every pattern shot.

Transposition of the tie-up for a pattern having combined spots may be more easily understood by a study of Fig. 113. The tie-up for the ordinary falling shed is shown at A; for a double tie-up on a loom having two sets of lamms, the harnesses tied to rise are marked O and those tied to fall are marked

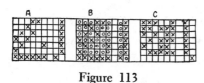

Figure 113

X at B of Fig. 113. The tie-up for a rising shed is shown at C of Fig. 113 and is seen to be exactly the opposite of A, and the same as the part marked O at B.

Types of yarns. Originally bronson was a weave for household linens and perhaps it is still most used for that purpose. It is the skips, whether warp or weft, that get the most wear and will break first with age. Many pieces which have come down from Colonial times have worn spots instead of overshots, so that the pattern seems to be made by holes in the tabby background, which is still intact. Naturally, the longer skips wear out most quickly; so the smaller skips are preferable in a piece of linen that is to be used. A better looking fabric as well as a better wearing one results if the warp and weft are of the same yarn; though the colors may differ.

Variations. It is amazing what a change of yarn and sley will do for spot bronson. Even a very simple pattern may be varied almost indefinitely in the treadling to give a wide variety of patterns. The spots may be used alone or they may be combined. The draft may be the usual four ends per unit, or it may be expanded to six, eight, ten or more ends per unit. In some variations, the unit may even be two ends. In most of these variations, it is the warp overshot side that is the usable side; many have long weft overshots which make the side they occur on ugly and useless.

A soft yarn, or several strands of a fine yarn used together, sleyed closely enough to give a warp-faced fabric, makes an excellent upholstery material. This calls for treadling a bit different from that usual for spot bronson. The rule of a multi-harness tabby at every alternate shot still holds, but there is an additional single-harness tabby. The basic form of the treadling is shown at Fig. 114; it does not show any combination of spots, nor a special tie-up. The fabric shown at Fig. 115 was woven of a six-

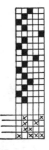

Fig. 114

strand mercerized cotton commonly called "floss." There are 10 ends per unit and 30 ends per inch. The pattern draft is the same as that shown at Fig. 106. The weft is a No. 3 perle but in a darker shade—color does little in this weave. The side of the fabric having the weft overshots is most unattractive.

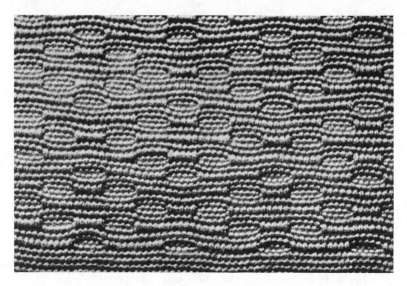

Figure 115

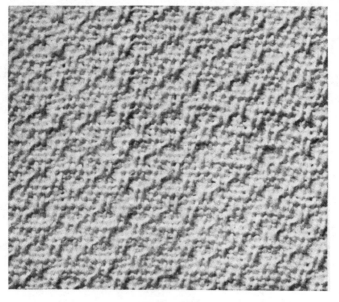

Figure 116

The threading draft as well as the pattern draft for Fig. 106 was used for the sample at Fig. 116. Here for both warp and weft 10/2 linen at 30 per inch was used. Only two wefts per unit were used, and the simple repeat of A, B, C was followed. Pattern, as such, is lost entirely, but the surface has a pebble effect. It is woven closely enough so that the texture is not lost when the fabric is stretched for upholstery.

The variations possible in spot bronson with just a change of yarn and sley are practically endless. The simplest variation and possibly the most obvious one is made by the use of two shuttles. Use a fairly hard-twisted yarn for warp and tabby weft, and a heavy soft wool for pattern weft. This weave is shown at Fig. 117. In the illustration, the warp and tabby are white in order to photograph well, but if both yarns are more nearly one color it is a much better looking fabric. It is suitable for a number of uses.

After the pattern shot is woven on the pattern combina-

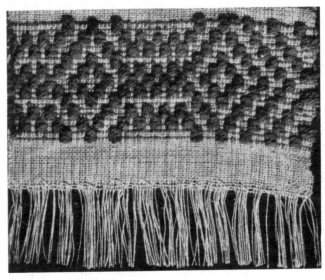

Figure 117

tion (1—2 or 1—3 or 1—4), a tabby is woven on the single-harness (#1) shed and then a second tabby is woven on the multiple-harness shed. In other words, both tabbies are woven after each pattern shot. The tabby on the single-harness shed weaves in the same shed with the background of the pattern weft, but the second tabby weaves in its own shed. There is no warp overshot on the under side of the fabric. The balance between the pattern weft and the foundation weft is most important, but a little experimenting will solve all problems that arise in establishing it.

A variation that is interesting especially from the design standpoint is illustrated at Figs. 118 and 119. This particular piece was made to be used as a pocket on an organdy apron and the design is used as a whole rather than as a repeat design. Repeat designs or a single unit used as decoration on a larger surface are just as easily done. This variation gives one a good chance for experimenting with "free form" in which the design is not so rigidly restricted by the mechanics of the loom.

At Fig. 118 it is shown that the design is a three-block one, following the rules of all block designs. At first glance, the black part of the design seems not to follow all rules, for sometimes the blocks are combined and sometimes they are ignored. This effect is accomplished in the treadling by a sort of "laid-in" technique, with the harnesses counting the warps instead of the weaver having to do it.

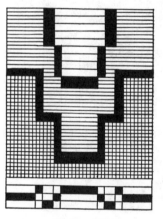

Figure 118

The harness that carries the warps for a pattern block makes a tabby shed with the first harness. To weave this laid-in pattern, raise the harness (or harnesses) that will

Figure 119

make a shed where the first color is to be, and put the proper
pattern shuttle through that short shed; raise the next pattern
shed and put that color through. Several shuttles of the same
color may be used to prevent long floats. For an all-over design
such as Fig. 118, there will be a pattern weft under every top shed
warp. Then change the shed to bring the #1 harness up, and
weave with a plain tabby.

If scattered spots of pattern are to be used, the pattern
weft goes in the shed at the proper intervals and *both* tabbies

are woven. This puts a tabby in the same shed with the pattern weft at the pattern spots.

This fabric is woven with the wrong side up. There are long floats, and sometimes reversing loops on the wrong side, so that it is not a usable side. This fabric should therefore be used for such articles as are lined or do not show both sides. The long floats may be cut off to reduce bulk, but the cut ends still look unattractive and sometimes catch and pull out. Fig. 119 is a detail of the weave.

PROBLEMS

1. Fig. 120 is a design taken from the ancient *Neuhervorkommendes Weber Kunst und Bild Buch von Nathaniel Lumscher* published in 1711, a copy of which is now in the print room of New York's Metropolitan Museum. Make a pattern draft for it. Make a threading draft to be woven in spot bronson.

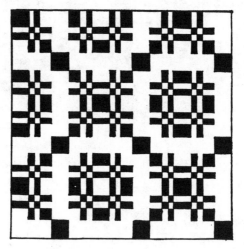

Figure 120

2. Fig. 121 is a pattern draft of a design from the same book. Make the pattern diagram, the threading draft, the tie-up and the treadling draft for it to be done in spot bronson.

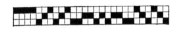

Figure 121

3. Make a six-spot pattern allowing for adjacent and alternate combinations of spots.
4. Adapt the above pattern to some definite object, such as a towel, a tablecloth, or bag material.

CHAPTER 8

Lace Bronson

Lace bronson, like all other weaves, is known by a number of different names: "lace weave," "open weave," "Swedish lace" and others. In the Scandinavian countries it is quite commonly called "curtain weave," and if there is no pattern, but if the entire fabric is lace, it is called "myggtjäll" or "mosquito net." The name "lace bronson" seems to have originated with Mrs. Atwater, when she introduced the weave after her study of the old Bronson book. Although Swedish lace and lace bronson are identical in structure, the methods of drafting and weaving them are quite different.

Apparent characteristics. Blocks of open lace-like effect form the pattern and the background is tabby. It is a two-thread construction—one warp and one weft. Pattern blocks and background are interchangeable. The pattern is identical on both sides, but the structure is slightly different; the overshots are weft on one side and warp on the reverse. As with spot bronson, this is the distinguishing characteristic.

Actually, lace bronson is made by a series of spots set next to each other; the separating or dividing warp between the spots is the warp that seems to stand out to make the bar effect in

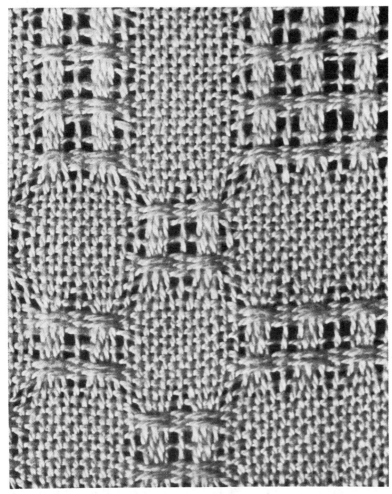

Figure 122

the open spaces. The pattern warps and the pattern wefts group together, but the separating threads stand by themselves (Fig. 122).

Structural characteristics in most instances are the apparent ones. A single block of lace consists of several spots joined so that the separating threads make the single crossbars which give the open, lace-like effect. As in spot bronson, every alternate warp thread is on the first or foundation harness. The separating threads are on a harness of their own and a separating thread follows every group of threads forming a spot. A single spot is repeated any number of times with its separating thread to form a single block of pattern. The warp threads for each block of the pattern, exclusive of the foundation and separating threads, are carried on their individual harnesses. With two harnesses reserved for foundation and separating threads, it naturally follows that a two-block pattern is possible on a four-harness loom, a four-block pattern on a six-harness loom, and so on. In order that the threads may group together and that the separating thread may have a chance to show itself separately, and so form a block of lace, there should be at least four spots in a block; that is, it should be two spots wide and two spots high. A single spot would remain a "spot" and would have no chance to become "lace."

Design. Even on a four-harness loom, lace bronson offers a wide variety of possibilities. It can be woven successfully in almost any material: wool, silk, cotton, or synthetic fibers, and for an endless number of articles. The size of the block need not be limited because of any practical or structural reasons, and the design can be varied amazingly.

The adaptability of lace bronson to household linens and to such articles of wearing apparel as scarves and mufflers makes one think immediately of initials. In this weave some letters can be done with two blocks of design and all can be done with four blocks. Often it is possible to combine two or three initials in one threading.

Fig. 123 shows some two-block letters. They are not all possible on the same threading, but a little planning when threading the loom will help that problem. A, H, O and U are

Figure 123

all done on the same set-up and C, E, F and L can be done on
another. M and W are done on the same threading, but I, T
and J require individual threadings. When threading the loom,
skip heddles on the harnesses not used so that they will be
ready if you want to change only a few warps to make a different letter. For instance, the H is threaded A block, B block, and
another A block. When threading for initials, the right hand A
is threaded 1-2-(empty 3)-1-2-(empty 3)-1-4. Later, the two
warps on the #2 harness are transferred to the ready and wait-
ing #3 heddles. Or, heddles on #4 may also be skipped and
later the warps rethreaded to make tabby background. If you
use string heddles, after they have served for an initial they may
be cut instead of the warp, and new heddles tied around the
warp. In this way, two or three or more letters may be woven
(vertically, of course) on the same fabric with no cut warp-ends.

Fig. 124 shows four-block letters made in the diagrammatic
representation used in Chapter 5. Fig. 125 shows some combinations of letters with their pattern drafts. Because the structure
of lace bronson is the same in both warp and weft, it does not
matter in which direction the letters are woven, as illustrated
in the combination H-T-B. What does matter is the direction

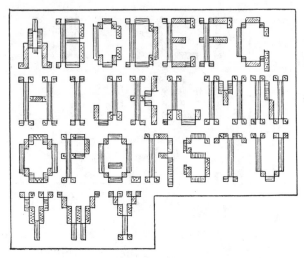

Figure 124

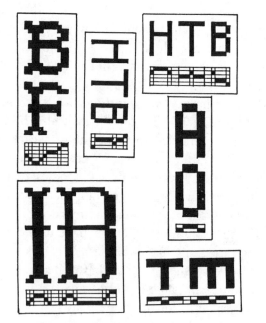

Figure 125

of the letters themselves. A, O, M and some others are the same in either direction, but such letters as E, L, and S must be planned carefully for placing on the fabric.

Draft writing. There are two methods of writing the draft for this weave. The simpler one is the American way, or the "lace bronson" way. The Swedish method is not quite so simple, but does have the advantage of working more easily on a counterbalanced loom.

The American method will be considered first; it may be applied to any number of harnesses—four or more. Lace bronson is made by a series of spots placed next to each other with separating threads between the spots. As in spot bronson, one harness is reserved for the foundation, usually the first harness, and one harness is assigned to the separating threads. The last harness is usually the separating harness, though quite often the second harness is used for this purpose. As in spot bronson, which harness is used is of no consequence, so long as the same harness is always used for that purpose in any one draft. In this book, the last harness will be used, whether it is the fourth, fifth, eighth or any other. Those weavers who are in the habit of using the second harness will have no trouble in transposing any draft so that the separating warp threads will be on the second harness.

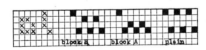

Figure 126

The separating warps if used with the foundation warps make plain cloth or tabby. Thus, on a four-harness loom, a selvage or plain weave border may be written 1-4-1-4-1-4 for any desired width (Fig. 126).

It will be noted that there are six threads in any unit.

Usually, six is the best number; four threads (1-2-1-4 or 1-3-1-4) in a unit do not allow for enough grouping of the threads in the finished fabric and the effect is "scratchy" rather than lace-like. Occasionally, on very coarse materials, a four-thread unit is permissible. If the article planned calls for a closely-woven tabby background and yet an open lace, two extra threads may be added to each unit, making a total of eight threads—three pattern, one separating, and four foundation threads. In order that there may be any kind of lace effect, there should be a minimum of two units in each direction (warp and weft) in any block of pattern.

No matter how many blocks in the pattern, the principle of draft writing is the same: three (or four) threads on the foundation harness, two (or three) threads on the pattern harness, and one thread on the separating harness. This means that alternating threads are on the foundation harness. The *units* of a draft for a four-harness pattern are shown at Fig. 126. Plain weave is considered in this case as a unit just as Blocks A and B are.

Tie-up. The principles governing the tie-up for lace bronson are exactly the same as for spot bronson. The foundation harness constitutes one tabby and the combination of all other harnesses makes the second tabby. A pattern harness plus the foundation harness is the combination used to produce a single block of pattern in the weaving. Two or more harnesses are combined with the foundation harness to weave a combination of two or more blocks. The only combination never used is the combination of foundation and separating harnesses. The tie-up for a loom with a rising shed is the opposite of that used for a falling shed in order to have the weft skip side of the fabric the visible side when it is on the loom.

Treadling for lace bronson, like that for spot bronson, follows the same order as the threading. Every alternate pick is a combination tabby shot, and every sixth pick is a separating thread on the single-harness tabby. If this treadling is followed on a falling shed loom, the weft overshots will be on the top or visible side of the fabric during the weaving. If the shed is a rising one, the warp overshots will be the visible ones. It is easier to count the weft overshots when they are visible, so ordinarily the tie-up that gives visible weft overshots is the one to use (Fig. 127).

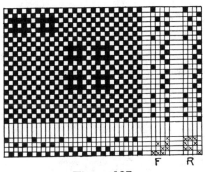

Figure 127

Ignoring the problem of which overshot is visible during the weaving process, the order of treadling for Block A would be 1—2, combination tabby, 1—2, combination tabby, single tabby (separating thread), combination tabby. If there are eight threads in each unit of the pattern draft, then of course there will be three pattern shots instead of two in each unit woven.

To weave the B block, 3—1 is substituted for 2—1. If there are more than two blocks in the design, C substitutes 4—1, D substitutes 5—1, and so forth.

Because the warps for each block of lace are carried on a single harness, these blocks may be combined to make larger blocks of lace. On a two-block pattern the two blocks may be combined to form a solid area of lace.

Figure 128

Fig. 128 shows three place mats and the pattern draft from which they are woven. The bottom mat is woven as drawn in, the black area being the lace pattern and the white the tabby background. In the center mat, Blocks A and B are combined to make the solid lace border; then the A block is woven to make a corner square of tabby; the combined blocks are again woven to make the narrow stripe and the A block alone makes the center section.

The top design is a "free form" sort of design and is more easily woven on the loom than it is described in words. It is a picked-up type of weave with the harness instead of the weaver counting the threads. Note that the lace is placed where it is set in the loom, but it is used only part of the time. This picked-up weave is not easily done on a counterbalanced loom. The loom should have a direct tie-up: harness 1 tied to treadle 1, harness 2 tied to treadle 2, and so on.

A simplified diagram is shown at Fig. 129. To weave section A: with the shuttle at the right, harness 1 is lowered and the shuttle passed to a point just before the wide A block begins (shown as x). Then harness 2 is lowered with harness 1, making 1—2 down to give the wide lace area and tabby to the selvage, and the shuttle is passed through this remaining part of the shed to the edge. The shuttle is *not* removed from the shed in the middle of the cloth but stays in the shed from selvage to selvage, no matter how many times the shed may be adjusted. Weave tabby on the 2-3-4 shed from left to right. Repeat the pick-up shed and the 2-3-4 tabby.

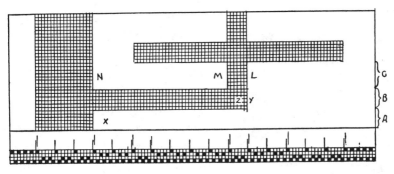

Figure 129

Then weave the #1-harness tabby to make the separating thread and follow with a 2-3-4 tabby. This makes six wefts to correspond with the six warp threads and gives one unit of design. This is repeated for the desired size.

To weave section B: harness 1 is lowered and the shuttle taken to a point just before the narrow A block (about at Y); harness 2 is also lowered to make the small A block, and the shuttle is taken to about the middle of the lace section (about at Z) and the #3 harness is also lowered, making harnesses 1-2-3 down and lace all the way through the wide A block; the shuttle is taken to the left selvage. Always the 2-3-4 shed means that the shuttle is from left to right; when the shuttle is from right to left, harness 1 is down with one or two other harnesses for pattern or alone for separating thread. There are two pattern shots and one separating shot from right to left and three three-harness tabbies from left to right.

The pick-up for section C is: harness 1 down and the shuttle to L; 1 and 2 down, shuttle to M; 1 down and shuttle to N; 1—2 down and shuttle to the edge. After a little practice, this form of pick-up goes very fast and makes design possibilities, even for four harnesses, almost limitless.

Fig. 130 is a four-block pattern; at the bottom it is woven

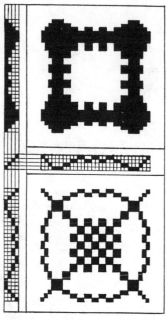

Figure 130

as drawn in and at the top the blocks have been combined to make a quite different-looking design. The black section is all lace and is achieved by the tie-up and the treadling. There is no pick-up in this design but it does call for a six-harness loom. The design could be used as a single unit rather than as a repeat. It would make an interesting luncheon cloth or in very fine linen it might even make a handkerchief. A threading draft with tie-up for 948 ends is given at Fig. 131.

There are several advantages to weaving this fabric by the American or "Bronson" draft. The draft is very easily written whether for four harnesses or for more; the tie-up is equally simple. The blocks may be combined, and there may be areas of plain weave through the width of the fabric as well as at the edges.

Normally, one side of the fabric has warp overshots and the reverse side has weft overshots. By an easy shift in treadling,

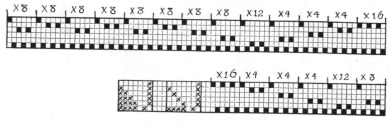

Figure 131

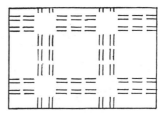

Figure 132

the direction of the overshot may be changed at will, so that the direction of the overshots may be as much a part of the design as the whole block itself. Fig. 132 is a diagrammatic representation of a checked cloth in which the horizontal stripes have weft over-shots and the vertical stripes have warp overshots. This feature is especially valuable in weaving with more than one color, for it makes the color value of all lace blocks the same. In Fig. 133 compare A with B.

The great disadvantage of the American method of writing the draft is that it is difficult to weave on many counterbalanced looms. The Swedish method of writing the draft overcomes this difficulty by making the tabby on the 1—3 and 2—4 combinations and the pattern shot on a single-harness shed. Only two of the six shots are on the unbalanced shed instead of the three tabby shots and the one separating thread.

The A block is written 1-2-1-2-1-4, and the B block is written 4-3-4-3-4-1. When progressing from one block to another, one must take care that two 4's do not come next to one another and that the 1 does not repeat. As in the American method, the selvage is written 1-4-1-4-1-4. The Swedish weaver is quite likely to group five ends in a dent and then skip dents on each side of the separating thread. This gives a striped effect to the tabby portions that is not always an added attraction.

The threading draft, tie-up, and treadling draft of the Swedish method are shown at Fig. 134. It is important when changing blocks to see that two wefts do not get in the same shed—both the 1—3 and the 2—4 tabbies must be used between blocks.

In the Swedish method, the blocks do not combine as they

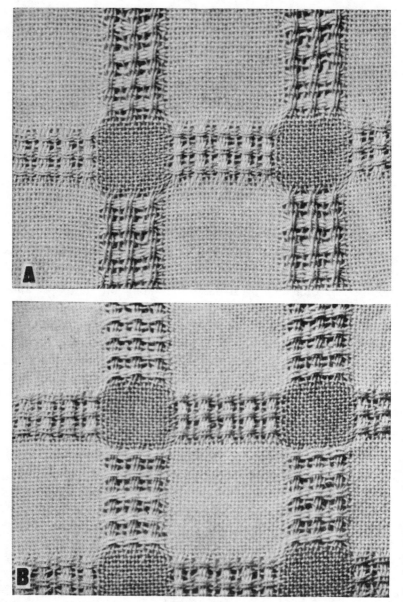

Figure 133

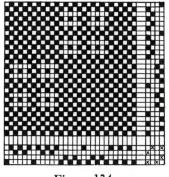

Figure 134

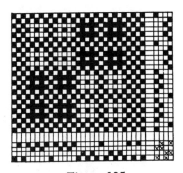

Figure 135

do in the Bronson method. When the blocks are combined, one block has warp overshots and the other block has weft overshots. This effect can be used to advantage; set the warps closer together so that the fabric will not be lace-like at all. There will be no tabby background, but there will be an all-over pattern—a sort of two-block damask effect caused by one block of warp overshots adjacent to one of weft overshots. See Fig. 135 for the draft and tie-up and see Fig. 136 for the effect of the weave.

It is well to remember that lace bronson is seldom attractive while it is on the loom. It takes at least one trip to the laundry before the threads, either warp or weft, group together to open up the lace part of the cloth. If the fabric is one that is not to be laundered severely (some wools), the lace can be encouraged by stretching the fabric diagonally and rubbing it as though it were being washed.

Sley is important in lace bronson. A rather open sley makes for more attractive lace, though of course the tabby part will be soft too. A good lace is made with 40/2 linen set at 24 per inch, the tabby is firmer and though the lace has lost much of its openness, it is not a fatal loss. At 36 or 40 per inch the tabby is practically sailcloth and the lace, even if there are

Figure 136

eight ends per unit, is hardly lace at all. In all instances, the beat is equally important. There should be as many picks as ends per inch. Lace bronson is very definitely a square weave.

PROBLEMS

1. Make a two-block pattern and write the drafts in both Bronson and Swedish methods.

2. Write the threading draft, the tie-up, and the treadling drafts for three or four different letters (initials).
3. Make a combination of two or more letters to be woven on a single threading.
4. Make a two-block design for a lace-bordered handkerchief with the overshots in both directions.
5. Make a "free form" design and weave it.
6. Make a Swedish draft for a two-block design and weave it in combined blocks.

CHAPTER 9

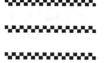

Summer-and-Winter Weave

Not much is known of the origin and early history of the summer-and-winter weave. We have usually considered it to be a distinctively American weave—our one contribution to the vast store of weaving knowledge. M's and O's, the bronsons, Colonial overshot, and all the other weaves have been found in many countries and through many ages, but summer-and-winter seems to stand alone as an early American accomplishment. In weaving books from Finland, we find drafts that are practically identical in general arrangement, but the fabrics woven on them have nothing in common with the woven summer-and-winter.

When a diagram analysis of summer-and-winter (without tabby threads) is compared with a diagram of damask (Fig. 137), some similarities are found. This has led to the theory, which may or may not be true, that it was the outgrowth of an attempt to weave damask on a less complicated loom than the ten harnesses required for even a simple two-block pattern.

Summer-and-winter seems to have been done in America from about the time of the Revolution. Since the patterns possible on a four-harness loom are definitely limited, it probably

130

was not a home weave but was the work of professional or semi-professional weavers. This new technique of the late eighteenth century had much to recommend it and as its popularity grew, new weavers added to its growing possibilities and patterns. With the introduction of the Jacquard loom to America in 1826, summer-and-winter went into a temporary eclipse.

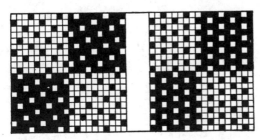

Figure 137

Regardless of its origin, summer-and-winter has much to recommend it in the mid-twentieth century as in the late eighteenth. It is a sturdy fabric suitable for many uses, and its design possibilities are definitely in step with the times.

Apparent characteristics. Summer-and-winter is a two-tone weave: there are pattern and background (Fig. 138). The cloth is reversible: one side shows a light pattern on a dark background and the other side shows a dark pattern on a light background. The texture on both sides may be identical, and if not identical, it is quite similar. Perhaps the fact that it could be used on both sides suggested its name—the light side for summer and the dark side for winter. Aside from the seasonal appearance, it must have been a great satisfaction to careful housewives that both sides could receive equal amounts of wear. The pattern is identical on both sides.

It is a three-thread construction: there is a warp, a pattern weft, and a tabby or binder weft. The tabby yarn is usually slightly finer than the warp and the pattern yarn is heavier.

Figure 138

The pattern is formed by blocks, and the blocks conform to all rules governing block patterns. An advantage to designing is that two or more blocks may be combined to make larger blocks. The many Pine Tree borders found on old coverlets are excellent examples of this.

There are no long overshots of pattern weft; the pattern blocks are made up of many small overshots. These pattern floats or skips are always over three warps and under one except at the edges of the blocks where some skips are over only two warps. The weft overshots are not parallel to each other, but alternate like bricks in a wall so that the warp thread that divides two small skips in one row of weft becomes the center one of three warps under the overshot in the following row. This is the distinguishing characteristic of summer-and-winter weaving. In no other type of handweaving do we find small overshots in a large block with this "brick wall" effect.

The pattern blocks may or may not have a warp thread in common where the corners of the blocks meet each other. This depends on the treadling and will be discussed under that heading.

Structural characteristics are the same as apparent characteristics because it is structure that makes appearance. The most important characteristic of all is a structural one which does not show in the cloth, but does make all of the other characteristics visible. This important characteristic is the arrangement of the warps on the harnesses, or more simply, the threading draft and the treadling draft. Two harnesses are reserved for the foundation of the cloth and each remaining harness carries the warp threads for a single block of pattern. Therefore a four-harness loom can weave a two-block pattern, a five-harness loom can weave a three-block pattern, a six-harness loom can weave a four-block pattern, and so on.

Designs for summer-and-winter have several advantages over designs for some other types of fabrics. Chiefly, the designer is not limited to any definite size of blocks lest the structure

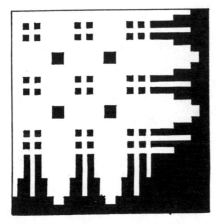

Figure 139

of the cloth be weakened or made impractical for use because of long skips. With the possibility of combining two or more blocks to make a larger block of irregular shape, the design becomes flexible. Summer-and-winter is a splendid medium for so-called modernistic designs. The corner of the tablecloth shown at Fig. 139 illustrates the combining of blocks and the contrasting of sizes.

The freedom of design resulting from the combining of blocks is further illustrated at Fig. 140. In the upper left is the simplest possible four-block pattern, which in itself is far from interesting. From it have been derived the other eleven designs—some good, some bad, and some just plain silly. In the top row the blocks have been combined to keep the diagonal appearance and in the middle row they have been combined to make horizontal and vertical lines. On the bottom row, more freedom and imagination have been used; a little imagination produced the pine trees in the third design; perhaps more than a little imagination plus a little trickery were used for the sailor boys in the last design.

With two-block designs, naturally the possibilities of combinations are decidedly limited, but the blocks may be combined, very often successfully (Fig. 141). With a more elaborate design than the very simple diamond of Fig. 140, although the principles and methods of combining blocks remain the same, the results are more interesting and vastly more varied. Fig. 142 is the pattern most commonly known in its Colonial overshot version as Honeysuckle. The combination making circles is neither interesting nor good; the two square designs are much better and if properly handled in summer-and-winter have decided possibilities as upholstery materials.

Draft writing for summer-and-winter is a very simple matter. The first requirement is a pattern draft. The threading draft is then applied by formula—the A block is written 3-1-3-2;

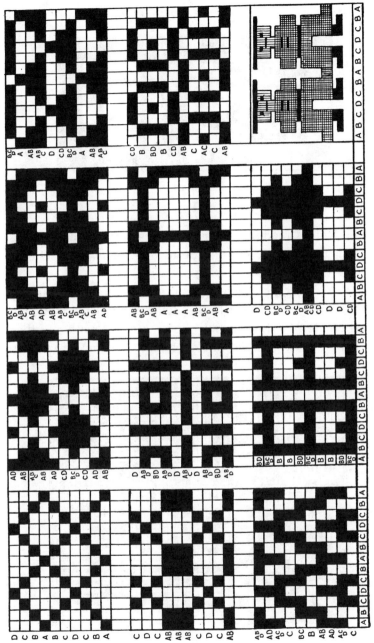

Figure 140

135

Figure 141

Block B is written 4-1-4-2; Block C is written 5-1-5-2. This method is the same for as many harnesses as the loom possesses. The four threads of each unit are used as many times as there are units in the block of the design.

The structural characteristics of summer-and-winter require that two harnesses be kept for the foundation of the fabric and that alternate warp threads must be on one or the other of these two harnesses; which two does not matter. Some weavers use

Figure 142

the two in the front of the loom, and others use the two in the back, or even the two middle harnesses of a six-harness loom. In this chapter harnesses 1 and 2 will always be considered the foundation harnesses, since all looms have a #1 and a #2 harness regardless of whether there are four or six or even more harnesses to carry the warp threads for the pattern blocks.

After the foundation harnesses are designated, the remaining harnesses are assigned, one to each block of the pattern. Thus the warp threads for the A block are on the #3 harness and the B blocks are on the #4 harness and so on as far as the pattern demands. Therefore the formula: Block A is written 3-1-3-2; Block B is written 4-1-4-2; Block C is 5-1-5-2, and so forth.

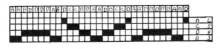

Figure 143

Fig. 143 is the *pattern draft* for the design at Fig. 75. Reading from the right, Block D is one unit wide, Block A is two units wide, Block B is five units wide, and so on. At Fig. 144 the pattern draft is written in rectangles rather than in squares and directly below it is the threading draft. The pattern draft for summer-and-winter is sometimes called the "short draft." Most weavers prefer to thread from the pattern draft, or short draft, rather than from the expanded threading draft, because it is easier to follow the simpler pattern (short) draft than the expanded draft and it is easier to check for mistakes. Each unit

Figure 144

square of the pattern draft represents four threads of warp drawn through the harnesses in the order of 4-1-4-2 or 3-1-3-2 or whatever the case may be. This is shown at Fig. 144.

Some drafts are written 4-2-4-1 instead of 4-1-4-2, or sometimes 1-4-2-4. This makes no difference in the finished cloth, but it does affect the treadling to a certain extent. Whatever the sequence used, it must be followed exclusively in any one draft. *Never* may a draft be written x-1-x-2 for one block and x-2-x-1 for another. In weaving there are many things that can be done equally well in more than one way, but it is of the utmost importance that the weaver be consistent in the use of any one method in a single piece of work.

The foregoing explanation of draft writing has been chiefly for four-block (and consequently six-harness) patterns. There is no difference in the principles governing the writing of drafts for any number of blocks and harnesses.

Tie-up. From the threading draft for summer-and-winter (Fig. 144), it is evident which harnesses must be used to produce tabby weave. And if corroboration is needed, the structural characteristics tell that alternate warps are on the first two harnesses. Therefore the tie-up for any summer-and-winter tabby weave is the two foundation harnesses against *all* of the pattern harnesses. No matter how many blocks in the pattern or how many harnesses, tabby weave is obtained by treadling alternately 1—2 against 3—4 on a four-harness loom or 1—2 against 3-4-5-6-7-8 on an eight-harness loom.

The blocks of a pattern are made up of small overshots of pattern yarn; these overshots in any single block are not all made by the same combination of harnesses. There are two separate and distinct rows of pattern shots in each block of pattern (Fig. 138). Looking at Fig. 144 one sees that the first pair of warps is 6—1 and that the second pair is 6—2. Each block of pattern is composed of two pairs of warps and these pairs are repeated as often as is necessary to form the required size of pattern block. In the combination of 6—1, there are three adjacent warps, which will make a small overshot. In the combination of 6—2 there are two adjacent warps. This tells then the combination of harnesses to be used for each block, namely: 6—1 and 6—2 for the D block, 3—1 and 3—2 for the A block. The tie-up for simple weaving for a six-harness loom is shown at A of Fig. 145.

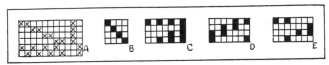

Figure 145

Just as the pattern draft is a short method of writing the threading draft, so there is a short method of writing the tie-up —B of Fig. 145. The tabby is not indicated. D block on the tie-up is a single black square, which means that the harness carrying the D block (or #6 harness) is tied to two pedals, each one of which has tied to it also one or the other of the foundation harnesses. This combining of one pattern harness with one foundation harness constitutes a simple tie-up for summer-and-winter weaving. A and B of Fig. 145 give exactly the same information; B is the pattern tie-up and A is the actual tie-up on the loom.

It will be noted that the simple tie-up for a four-harness loom is the standard tie-up. While the combinations of harnesses are the same in both cases, it is important to note that 1—2 and 3—4, which are pattern combinations in the standard tie-up, become tabby in summer-and-winter and that the standard tabby combinations of 1—3 and 2—4 become pattern combinations.

For those patterns in which the blocks are combined the principle of the tie-up is the same as for a simple tie-up: two or more pattern harnesses, as needed, are used with each of the two foundation harnesses. In the designs in Fig. 142, the tie-up for the design in the upper left corner is a simple one, each block being used separately. To produce the pattern in the upper right, the draft is the same but a different tie-up is necessary. Block D is the only block that is ever used alone; Blocks A and D are combined for part of the pattern; Blocks A, B, and D for another part; and finally, for the horizontal lines that go entirely across the pattern, all four blocks are used in combination. This is shown at C of Fig. 145.

It is hardly necessary to point out that the tie-up for the circular design is at D and that E is the tie-up for the design in the lower right corner. All of these tie-ups require ten treadles.

Treadling. Summer-and-winter is a three-thread fabric. A tabby shot must follow every pattern shot. By varying the order of treadling, two quite different-appearing fabrics may be obtained. At Fig. 146 are shown in detail four samples of summer-and-winter weaving. The two samples at the left (A and B) are woven as drawn in, or singly, or by the one and one method, three different ways of saying the same thing. The two samples on the right (C and D) are woven in pairs. There is no difference in the texture of the two samples woven as drawn in; the difference is in the way the blocks join at the corners. In the two samples of paired weaving there is an apparent difference in structure.

There are four warp-ends in each unit of design and theoretically there should be four weft threads in a unit—two pattern wefts and two tabby wefts. However, this does not always hold true in summer-and-winter weaving. Sometimes the block will weave square by adjusting the size of the weft yarns, but more often it is better to weave the block to the desired size, regardless of the actual count of the weft shots. When weaving

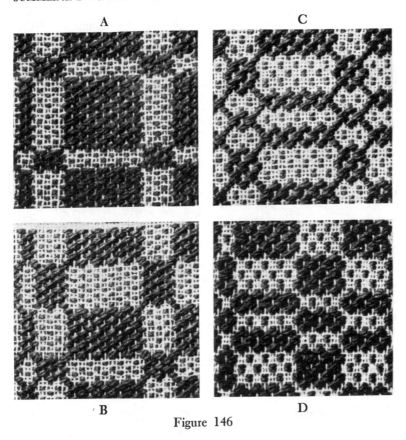

Figure 146

in pairs, four pattern and four tabby shots are needed to make
a single unit; and yarn adjustment, amount of beat, and the
number of units woven may all be involved in making the
pattern look as it should look, regardless of how it was planned.
This is always an individual problem and must be adjusted for
each piece of weaving while it is on the loom.

Fig. 147 is a diagram analysis of summer-and-winter woven
as drawn in. The tabby is *not* inked in; the diagram is of pattern
wefts only. There are several interesting features in this diagram.
One very noticeable thing is that while the pattern blocks have

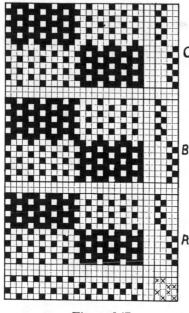

C

B

A

Figure 147

the required number of pattern shots (six pattern wefts to correspond with six pattern warps) the blocks are not really square. Probably in actual weaving, with the addition of the six tabby shots, the blocks would be square. Or it might be necessary to add two more pattern wefts, depending on the size of the yarns used.

In the first weft shot of the dark pattern block of section A there are three weft overshots that skip three warp-ends each. In the second pick there are only two overshots that cover three warp-ends, but there are at each side of the block two smaller skips which combine to make a third small overshot which belongs in that row. This is always true of all blocks in summer-and-winter—the edges of the blocks along the warp direction have a saw-tooth appearance, never a clear-cut straight line.

Still in the A section, another very noticeable thing is the almost straight line dividing the pattern block from the background in the weft direction. The first shot of the second pattern block is the direct opposite of the preceding pattern shot.

In section B, the most noticeable change in appearance is the exaggerated saw-tooth effect of the division between pattern and background in the weft direction. It also differs from A in that the blocks join each other at the corners in a twill effect. The treadling draft explains these changes in appearance.

In the B section the pattern blocks have an *odd* number of pattern shots so that the first and the last shots in each block are the same. Furthermore, this beginning and ending shot is on that combination of harnesses which will produce the two small skips at the edges of the blocks.

Section C is not very different from section B; the only change is that the background spaces join in the twill effect and thus the blocks are completely separated from each other. The treadling draft will explain this. It should be noted here that in actual weaving it does not matter whether the method at B or at C is used. One side of the cloth will show the effect at B and the other side will show the effect at C. But, as in threading, whichever sequence of treadling is chosen, that sequence must be used consistently. The order of treadling to use when weaving as drawn in depends to a great extent on the personal taste of the weaver and the ultimate use to which the fabric is to be put.

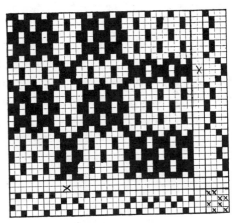

Figure 148

Fig. 148 shows a diagram analysis of summer-and-winter woven in pairs, and again the tabby wefts have been omitted to simplify the diagram. In this particular diagram, the blocks meet each other on a twill by starting with the picks containing the two-thread skips at each end of the pattern blocks. By starting with the three-thread skips, the blocks would have been as separate as the blocks of Fig. 147C. The treadling draft shows that it takes four weft shots to make a single unit of design or a *pair* of each pattern combination. In the diagram two units of the A block are woven first. The block starts with 3—2, then a pair of 3—1, followed by the second weft of the 3—2 pair. Weaving by units is sometimes confusing. It is much easier to say: start with a single shot, weave in pairs to the desired size, finish with a single shot to complete the pair which started the block. Single units (marked X on the diagram) are very likely to lose their identity and appear as mere transitions between two other blocks. Particularly is this true of two-block patterns, and this is a point to remember when one is making a design or a draft. If the pairs of wefts are not split at the beginning and the end of a block, the blocks will join each other in a way similar to those of Fig. 147A.

In Fig. 146, although C and D appear to be very different in texture, actually they are two sides of the same piece of cloth. In C the pairs are very obviously separated by the tabby, while in D the pairs are so close as to seem to be single shots of double-size weft. C is usually considered to be the right side of summer-and-winter. The difference in appearance is due to the *relation* of the tabby weft to the pattern weft. Usually the right side of the cloth will be the top or visible side while the fabric is on the loom if the foundation tabby (1—2) is used between the pairs and the tabby formed by the combination of all pattern harnesses is used in the center of each pair. This cannot be given as a rule to follow for there are too many circumstances, especially on a four-harness loom, which will alter the situation. The safest plan is to weave ten or twelve picks; then, if the pattern is wrong side up, simply put in an extra tabby weft—that is, have two tabbies next to each other—then go on with the regular treadling. This simple trick will immediately change the relation of the 1—2 tabby to the pattern weft and will turn the cloth right side up. The sequence of pattern treadling is not disturbed.

By far the best way to weave summer-and-winter, as well as all harness techniques, is to have the right side of the cloth the visible side. Do not memorize the treadling, nor even have the treadling draft written out for constant reference, but study well and know thoroughly the appearance of the pattern as a whole and of the various sheds in particular. Memory can fail and it is easy to skip a mark if the eyes have to travel back and forth from loom to notes. But if you watch each weft as it goes in and its relation to the previous one, mistakes are almost impossible. If the eyes check on the pattern and the weaving, the mind is free to plan dozens of things to be done next.

Variations. We do not, as a rule, think of summer-and-winter as a texture weave, but by ignoring its possibilities as such, we have been robbing ourselves of a vast source of variation in texture. The fact that there is never a skip of more than three warps makes summer-and-winter almost a twill threading (Fig. 149). Even with smooth yarns, summer-and-

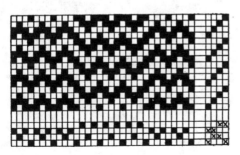

Figure 149

winter when woven as a twill can be interesting if there is variation in the size of the blocks. Needless to say the texture will
have more meaning in a heavy yarn. Be careful with the sley:
if the warp is to hold its identity and not be overpowered by
the weft, it must be sleyed more closely than for the orthodox
method of pattern weaving. The twill treadling at Fig. 149 is
only one of dozens that are possible. With color or texture or
both in warp and weft, the possibilities are endless.

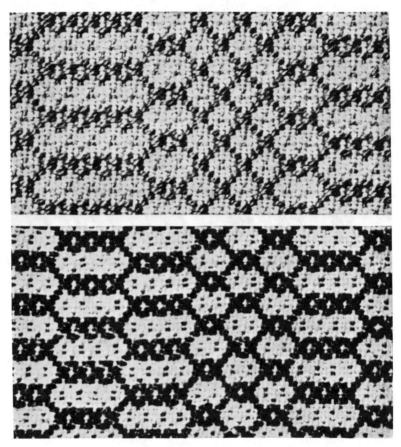

Figure 150

Figure 151

The most obvious variation for summer-and-winter is, of course, variation in pattern by the rearranging of the blocks to make different effects. Not too much rearranging is possible in a two-block design, but the pattern need not be followed as pattern. Fig. 150 shows the same treadling on two different threadings, neither of which has any remote resemblance to a bedspread, but both of which make successful upholstery fabrics.

The fact that each block of pattern is carried on its own harness and that blocks may be woven individually or in combination allows for great leeway in the use of color. On a two-block, four-harness pattern the use of two colors can change the entire appearance of the fabric. The whole surface has the same texture and there is no feeling of "background" (Fig. 151). The treadling for this method of weaving is given at Fig. 152. The group at X is for weaving as drawn in and the group at Y is for weaving in pairs. *Note* that the dark color is always considered the pattern color whether the pattern be on Block A or on Block B.

When the pattern is of more than two blocks, the possibilities are greatly increased. For instance, in Fig. 142 the design at the lower right can be done in only two colors, for the blocks overlap in such a way that neither of the two component parts of the design is completely independent of the other: to make one of them in any color requires that the other part be the same color. The design at the upper right is a different matter. The D blocks make the vertical enclosing lines and the combination of all blocks makes the horizontal lines. These lines can be a color to themselves. The pattern then has two colors, and the background can be the regular summer-and-winter background or it can be a third color (Fig. 153).

With this polychrome type of weaving, it is more than ever important to keep a good balance between yarns. And, too, the sley must be just right. There may be two or three pattern wefts before a tabby weft is entered. If the sley is too

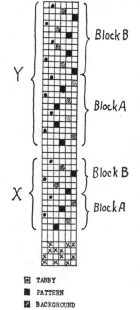

Y { Block B / Block A

X { Block B / Block A

▣ TABBY
■ PATTERN
▨ BACKGROUND

Figure 152

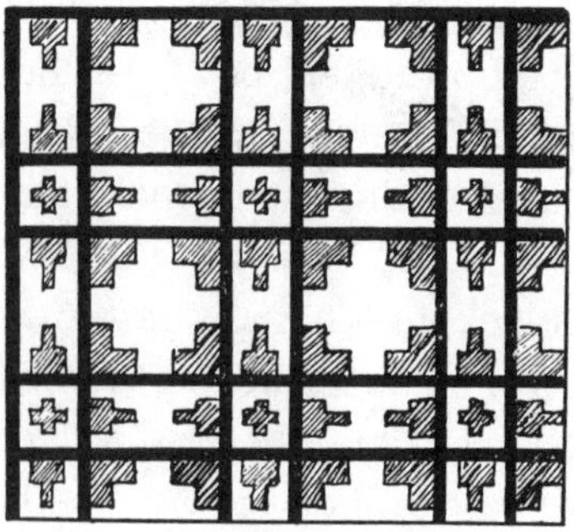

Figure 153

Figure 154

close and the pattern yarns too heavy, the balance of the fabric can be completely lost. As a rule, polychrome will need a slightly more open sley than will regular weaving. If the design is right and the colors are carefully handled, this type of weaving makes excellent upholstery material.

Bound weaving is that form of weaving in which the weft completely covers the warp. Bound weaving may be done on almost any type of draft, though of course it is more successful on some than on others. Summer-and-winter is one of the less successful; on four-harness looms there are only two blocks and design changes are decidedly limited, and on multi-harness looms there are not usually enough treadles.

The simplest bound weaving on summer-and-winter is woven on opposites. It may be done as drawn in or in pairs. It makes a stiff heavy fabric of limited use—probably best suited for rugs. Patterns for bound weaving are not too different from those done in polychrome (Fig. 154). Bound weaving has a more three-dimensional effect, for there is no tabby to keep the surface level.

The warp must be sleyed openly enough to let the wefts pack down well and completely cover the warp. By the elimination of the tabby shots from the treadling draft at X of Fig. 152, it becomes a treadling draft for weaving on opposites. The four shots for Block A are repeated till that block is large enough, then the four shots of Block B are repeated. Without the tabby, this is bound weaving on opposites.

Bound weaving in pairs is treadled differently from polychrome minus tabby. The proper sequence for treadling in paired opposites is given at Fig. 155. Note that there are eight shots needed to weave a single unit of either Block A or Block B; these eight shots of unit are repeated till the block is the required size.

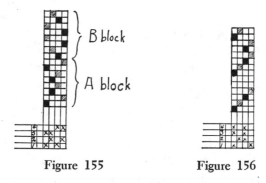

Figure 155   Figure 156

To combine blocks for a band of solid color, the combination of 1-3-4 is used for one color and is followed by a shot of a second color on the opposite shed, which is 2 alone. Then the combination of 2-3-4 is followed by 1 alone (Fig. 156).

Picked-up patterns are more a problem in design than in weaving. The weaving may be done either singly or in pairs

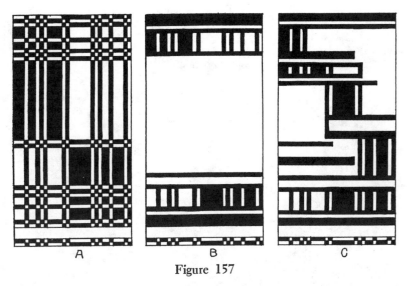

Figure 157

and with a tabby. It may be done in the polychrome type of weaving or in the bound weaving type. It is not a weave for which the treadling draft may be written and then followed blindly to the end of the piece. It takes thought and attention, but it is worth the effort. The weaving method is not too different from the picked-up method of lace bronson, already described.

Fig. 157 shows the development of a design for picked-up weaving. At A is a two-block pattern; at B is a design for a rug using the blocks plus combinations of the blocks for borders at the two ends. At C is a design using the blocks picked out where they are needed to make a modern design. The pattern draft is given under each design.

Fig. 158 is a sample woven on the pattern draft of Fig. 157. The lower part is woven as drawn in and the upper part is woven in pairs. Fig. 159 shows a sample woven according to parts of the design in C of Fig. 157. It is treadled as drawn in and is woven with a tabby.

Figure 158   Figure 159

The picked-up type of summer-and-winter is much easier if the loom is dressed to a single tie-up. Have harness 1 tied to treadle 1, harness 2 to treadle 2, and so on. Harnesses 1 and 2 are the foundation harnesses; harness 3 is the A block harness, and 4 is the B block. If the weft threads follow a fixed pattern of direction in relation to the treadles, it will be much easier than trying to remember which combination of harnesses comes next. For instance, in Fig. 160, at A, harness 1 is tied to treadle 1 on the left. To weave tabby, when the shuttle is on the left, use treadles 1 and 2; when the shuttle is on the right, use treadles 3 and 4. To weave Block A, pull down harnesses 1 and 3 and weave from left to right, then lower harnesses 2 and 3 and weave right to left. This, of course, is for falling shed; it is easier to think in terms of harnesses directly related to blocks. When the technique is mastered, the treadling may be transposed for a rising shed if desired. When the shuttle is on the right, use the treadle on the right with its proper partner (4 plus 3 for tabby and 2 plus either 3 or 4 for pattern); when the shuttle is on the left, use the left treadle with its proper partner. This practice makes treadling easier. B of Fig. 160 shows the same method, but the treadles are numbered from right to left.

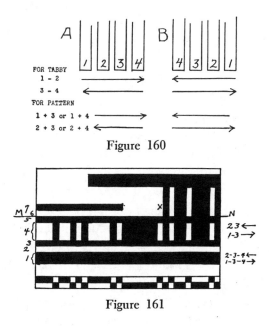

Figure 160

Figure 161

A diagrammatic scheme for weaving the design at Fig. 159 is given at Fig. 161. There are no problems before the line at M—N. If the treadles are arranged as at A of Fig. 160, to weave the first section, harnesses 1-3-4 are down and the shuttle is thrown from left to right; tabby; 2-3-4 down and weave from right to left; tabby. This is repeated for the proper distance.

For section 2 lower harness 1 only and weave from the left; tabby; harness 2 down and weave from the right; tabby. Every pattern weft is followed by its proper tabby. Section 3 is the same as section 1. In section 4, the A blocks only are woven. Section 5 is the same as section 1 and 3.

To weave section 6: if the shuttle is at the left, lower harness 1 only and take the shuttle to a point in the white space above the B block. Do not remove the shuttle from the shed; the harnesses are changed while the shuttle is in the shed and the shuttle is moved from point to point until it has gone completely across from one edge to the other. Holding harness 1 down, bring 3 down also; this automatically gives background at the X section and above all the other B sections to the edge. Take the shuttle to the edge. Weave a tabby. The pattern shuttle is at the right; so harnesses 2 and 4 are lowered and the shuttle again taken to X; harness 3 is released leaving only the 2 down, and the shuttle is taken to the left edge. Weave a tabby. These two pattern shots and two tabby shots are repeated as many times as the design calls for.

To weave section 7: the shuttle is at the left; harnesses 1-3-4 are lowered to combine both blocks and the shuttle is taken to a point just before the beginning of the large A block; harness 3 is released, leaving 1—4 down to give pattern at the small B block and background at the large A block; the shuttle is taken just beyond the right edge of the large A block where the shed is again changed to 1—3 to give pattern sheds on the A blocks to the right edge. Tabby. To return to the left selvage, the first shed is 2—3, changed to 2—4, changed to 2-3-4.

The weaving is really simpler than it sounds. When the shuttle is on the left, the left foot is on the pedal of the #1 harness and stays there for the complete passage of the shuttle from left to right; the right foot changes the shed as needed. When the shuttle is on the right, the left foot is on the pedal to hold down the #2 harness, and stays there while the right foot again changes the shed as needed. The shuttle does not leave the shed between selvages. After a little practice, the right foot will move from one treadle to another easily and the changes of shed will be determined by appearance rather than by reference to the number of the harness being raised or lowered. This pick-up weave can be done either as drawn in or in pairs.

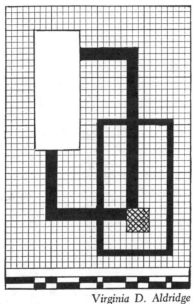

Virginia D. Aldridge

Figure 162

Polychrome and picked-up make an interesting combination, particularly for wall hangings in which the surface should all be of the same texture and color alone makes the pattern and background. Fig. 162 shows a design for a wall hanging done in black, white, gray, and red. It was woven in the direction shown in the illustration with the pattern draft, but hangs horizontally.

Virginia D. Aldridge

Figure 163

The possibilities of summer-and-winter are practically limitless. It may range from fine and soft textural weave to the sturdiest of rugs; its patterns may progress from the simple checkerboard through innumerable stages to "pictures" of trees and houses; it may very frankly look "bedspready" like its ancestor or it may set tomorrow's styles. Whatever its origin, its development has been American and American handweavers can well be proud of it and their pleasure in working with and developing it.

PROBLEMS

1. Write the pattern draft for Fig. 139.
2. Write the threading draft, tie-up, and treadling for Fig. 139.
3. Make a two-block design for a table mat using combined blocks.
4. Set up the loom with a two-block pattern and weave it according to the three methods of Fig. 147.
5. Weave the same design in polychrome.
6. Make a design for a selected pick-up weave such as Fig. 159.
7. Weave that design.
8. Plan and weave an upholstery fabric on a summer-and-winter draft.
9. Use a summer-and-winter draft to achieve a textured effect.

CHAPTER 10

Crackle Weave

Crackle is the name that was given to "Jämtlandsväv" when it was introduced to American handweavers. In Sweden some weaves are known by the names of the provinces where they supposedly originated or where they are extensively used. It was supposed that the Swedish name was too difficult for American weavers to pronounce, and that the background looked like the crackles in pottery glazes. Both suppositions seem rather far-fetched, but unfortunately the name of crackle has stuck and is still the generally accepted name for this valuable though not too often used weave.

Apparent characteristics. Crackle is a three-thread construction; there are a single warp and two wefts—a pattern weft and a tabby weft. It is a two-tone weave, having pattern and background. Fig. 164 shows a detail of the weave, or construction, of the cloth. The pattern blocks are made up of small overshots—the pattern wefts going over three warps and under one. These overshots are parallel, one above the other, so that the pattern blocks have a columnar or corded effect. The background is mostly tabby, but with added small spots of pattern weft also in straight lines. The structure of the cloth is the same on both

158

sides, but the pattern reverses: what is pattern on one side becomes background on the other side.

The distinguishing characteristic of crackle is one of pattern more than of structure. The *blocks* combine in a twill effect. In some other weaves the blocks may be combined as the designer wishes, but in crackle the blocks combine as would single warps in a twill weave.

Structural characteristics, of course, are the same as apparent characteristics, for it is the structure that makes the pattern and gives it its individual appearance. It is a three-thread construction. The pattern weft passes over three and under one warp to form the pattern blocks and reverses itself to form the background. There are occasions when the pattern

Figure 164

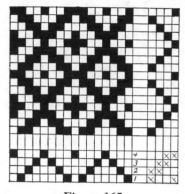

Figure 165

weft passes over or under two warp threads. Structurally, this two-warp skip occurs only between two blocks as they are threaded in the loom, but it shows, not at the edges of a pattern block, but on the surface of the block. If the pattern draft is a broken twill, the two-warp skip may or may not show up at the edges of the blocks.

Not only in pattern, but also in structure, crackle is a twill weave. Each block of pattern is composed of a series of point twills on three harnesses. But this is a matter of draft writing.

Design. Since it is the design or pattern as well as the structure that is the outstanding characteristic of crackle, an understanding of the design helps to make easier the understanding

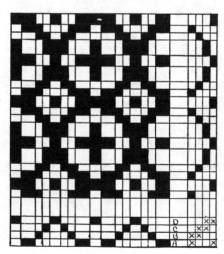

Figure 166

of the other characteristics. While the design is usually a four-block pattern, the blocks do not meet at the corners, but combine to make a twill. If the pattern of any crackle weave is considered merely as an enlarged twill, it immediately loses all its mystery and confusion.

The twill effect of the pattern is shown at Fig. 165 and Fig. 166. In Fig. 165 rosepath is woven as drawn in. Each square of the diagram represents *one* thread, whether warp or weft. In Fig. 166 the squares no longer represent single threads, but groups of threads, or *blocks* of a pattern and are named A, B, C, and D rather than 1, 2, 3, and 4 as they would be for threads. Also, the sizes of the blocks are not all the same as is the case with threads. The *blocks* weave together in the same twill combinations as though they were threads. A and B weave together just as 1 and 2 weave together; B and C combine as do 2 and 3; C and D combine as do 3 and 4; and A and D as do 1 and 4.

Blocks in crackle cannot be combined arbitrarily as they can be in the bronsons or in summer-and-winter, but *must* combine in the same combinations as a standard twill. A and C do not combine, nor do B and D.

The most notable thing about the blocks in a crackle pattern is that the blocks in the vertical rows keep their separate identities; there may be two, three, or any number of blocks woven adjacent to each other, but always each vertical row contains only its own block (Fig. 167). This is not true of the horizontal rows; each horizontal row is made up of a combination of two pattern blocks. Fig. 167 is the same pattern as Fig.

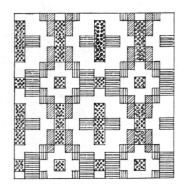

Figure 167

166, but the blocks in Fig. 167 are represented by their diagrammatic symbols. This illustration explains more clearly than words how all blocks in any vertical row are the same, and how in any horizontal row two pattern blocks are combined.

Fig. 168 is a design made for a rug; it is not a repeat design but a single pattern to fill the entire space. In it the D block is woven alternately with the A and C to make the continuous line in the center and at the edges.

Crackle designs should be kept simple. In spite of its valuable structure, crackle has not been used very extensively, and this is probably because of existing designs, so many of which are definitely out of step with modern styles. The patterns have a tendency to sprawl all over the place and to look

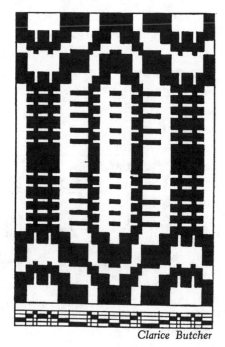

Clarice Butcher

Figure 168

Figure 169

Figure 170

"busy." Because of the type of draft they are of necessity large patterns, and the bisymmetric tendency of so many designs and the twill effect make for monotony.

Fig. 169 is a small design developed from the huck draft and Fig. 170 is another development of rosepath (compare it with Fig. 167) but even these, small as they are, will have to be developed in well-chosen yarns to be of any real value or great interest.

More than with most weaves, yarns must be considered when making the design for crackle. Plain flat yarns are rarely interesting, on the other hand strong contrast in color is what makes many crackle fabrics homely. Crackle is best when pattern and background are of nearly equal color value and when pattern is subordinated to texture.

A broken twill in the pattern draft and the design woven *not* as drawn in will help to make crackle a more interesting fabric. Fig. 171 is a three-block pattern—there is no D block

Figure 171

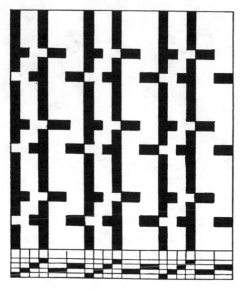

Figure 172

threaded in the loom. Even though it is treadled as drawn in, the break in the twill (C next to A) and the absence of a D block make an interesting pattern. The B—C combination weaves the horizontal bands of the large square. To weave the vertical wall of the square the combination of C—D is used, but because there is no D in the threading, naturally only the C block will show in the weaving. The four squares that touch the corners of the large squares are A blocks. No block can be woven alone; so the A blocks must be woven by the A—D combination, and again since there is no D block in the threading, the A block shows alone. The combination of A—B is not used.

Fig. 172 is a four-block broken twill pattern that is not woven as drawn in. The B—C combination is not used. The same pattern draft when woven as drawn in is just another mixture of meaningless rectangles.

The compulsory combination of blocks in a twill effect is not always an advantage. There are times when the sharp outlines of corner meeting corner make more contrast and more interest in a design. Such a design is shown at Fig. 173. In the pattern draft the blocks do not progress in an unbroken sequence throughout the entire draft. There is a B block next to a D block. In crackle the B and D blocks cannot be combined, nor can the A and C. Because they cannot be combined, they may be placed next to each other, and in the weaving the blocks meet corner to corner.

Draft writing. As in all other weaves, there is a formula for writing the draft. Each unit of the block is composed of four ends. The four ends make a point twill on three harnesses (Fig. 174).

When writing the threading draft for crackle, Block A is written with two threads on the #1 harness, one thread on the following harness, #2, and one thread on the preceding harness, which is #4. Simplified, this means that Block A is written 1-2-1-4. It is not necessary that these four threads come in this particular order; the order may be 4-1-2-1 or even 2-1-4-1.

Figure 173

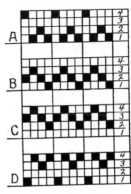

Figure 174

The order in which the threads come may be a personal choice, or may be dictated by the sequence of threads in the preceding block. But as always, when writing any draft, whatever order is chosen, that order must be used consistently.

Some weavers consider the 1-2-3-2 twill as the A block and the 1-2-1-4 as the D block. Again, this is a matter of choice so long as the same group is always used for the A block or the D block throughout the entire draft. It seems more logical, however, and much easier, to place the A block on the #1 harness, the B block on the #2 harness, the C block on the #3 harness and the D block on the #4 harness.

In the group of four threads making one unit of A block, two are on the #1 harness or 1-2-1-4. In the B block there are two threads on the second harness or 1-2-3-2. The C block is on the third harness or 2-3-4-3 and the D block is 4-3-4-1.

There are four rules for writing a crackle draft. If these are followed the draft will work correctly.

Rule 1. A thread on harness 1 must never come next to a 3, nor a 2 next to a 4. Crackle is a twill type of weave and to put 1 and 3 or 2 and 4 next to each other would make a break in the twill sequence and would spoil the tabby, which is essential for the binder weft. And just as obviously, two threads must not be together on any one harness.

Rule 2. The three-harness character of the point twills must be kept at all times. In order to keep the twills moving smoothly, it is sometimes necessary to add one, two, or possibly three extra threads to the draft. These extra threads are called accidentals. If the draft is becoming too long by the addition of accidentals, one, two, or three threads may be eliminated rather than added.

Rule 3. Never must there be more than three threads on any two adjacent harnesses. That is to say, there must never occur such a sequence as 1-2-3-2-1-2-1-4, for the 2-1-2-1 makes four threads together on the adjacent #1 and #2 harnesses. A similar mistake might be 4-3-2-3-4-3-4-1; or it might be a temptation to write 1-2-3-2-3-4-3-2. Obviously these four threads together would make a skip of four warps in the woven fabric, and according to the apparent and structural characteristics, the overshots or floats in crackle are always over three warp threads, except occasionally when they are over two warps at the transition of one block to the next.

Rule 4. Never may there be more than four threads in sequence before the direction of the twill changes. In transition from one block to the next, there will always be four threads in an unbroken sequence, but there must never be more than four. This rule is more simply stated thus: the sequence of 1-2-3-4 (or 4-3-2-1) must come between the B and C blocks, but never anywhere else, assuming that the B block is 2-3-1-2 and the C block is 2-3-4-3. If threading drafts could be written above and below the staff as is done in music, this sequence of four threads in any direction between blocks would be seen more clearly. An attempt to show this is made at Fig. 175.

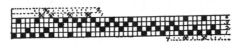

Figure 175

The harnesses above and below the staff are done in dotted lines and the threads on them are marked by X as well as in the regular way.

To write the draft for any given pattern the first requirement is a pattern draft. Then the formula for each unit is applied to the pattern draft as in any other type of weave. In the bronsons and in summer-and-winter there are no irregularities to bother about. In writing a crackle draft, while applying the unit groups of four threads to each pattern draft, one must keep in mind the four rules; sometimes the order of threading a unit is changed or accidentals added or a thread dropped.

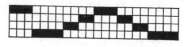

Figure 176

Fig. 176 is a pattern draft for the rosepath adaptation shown at Fig. 166. There are four units of A, two of B, two of C, three of D, which is the center or reverse block, and the pattern ends with another group of three units of D. The threading draft is written by starting with four repeats of the A block (Fig. 177); next come two repeats of the B unit. There are no problems thus far. An accidental on harness 1 must be added so that the sequence of 1-2-3-4 will come between the B and C blocks and to abide by Rules 1 and 3. In the draft at Fig. 177, the accidentals are represented by circles rather than by solid squares.

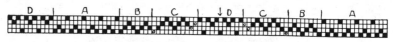

Figure 177

In the transition from Block C to Block D, there may be an accidental on harness 2, and the D block written 3-4-1-4. Or 2-3-4 may be considered the accidentals and the D block written 1-4-3-4. The choice will depend on whether or not the block may be three threads larger without spoiling the pattern.

This is a bisymmetrical pattern with the D block in the center of the repeat. The thread on the #1 harness is the center of the block. From this center thread (marked with an arrow) the draft is copied in reverse. In a bisymmetrical pattern it is always a good idea to copy the second half of a design from the first half. If the draft is written without regard to the first half, it is very easy to add or subtract two or three threads and throw the whole pattern off balance. A difference of six or eight or more threads in the two sides of a design makes a real change in the pattern, but a difference of two threads is just enough to be obvious as the mistake that it is.

At the end of the draft, the transition from A to D is correctly possible only by writing 1-2-1-4-3-4.

Although two-block patterns are practically nonexistent in crackle (summer-and-winter is a better weave for two-block patterns), they are possible. Whether two, three, or four blocks are used, crackle is always a four-harness weave, and all four harnesses must be used. Fig. 171, as previously noted, is a three-block pattern. The pattern draft is given at Fig. 178 and the threading draft is developed at Fig. 179. Because this is a three-block pattern, it comes in the general class of a broken twill—Block C is next to Block A.

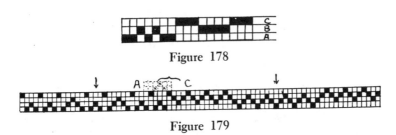

Figure 178

Figure 179

In writing the draft for a broken twill pattern, Rule 4 does not apply. Between A and C or between B and D, there must of necessity be five threads before the direction of the twill changes. In Fig. 179, the center of the large B block and the center of the small A block are indicated by arrows. The transition from C to A is shown with dotted lines above the staff, and X is used instead of the usual black squares. Between the A and the C are five threads, 2-3-4-1-2, in the same direction of twill.

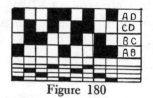

Figure 180

Figure 181

Fig. 180 is not a design that would make an acceptable woven fabric; it is done to show how the blocks combine when placed in regular and in broken sequence. What would be the threading draft is given at Fig. 181. The brackets at the top of the draft enclose the five threads that are the normal and necessary transition between blocks when those pattern blocks are in a broken twill sequence. The brackets at the bottom of the draft enclose the four-thread transition between blocks when the blocks are in a regular twill sequence.

Tie-up. In a crackle draft, it is easy to see that the tabby is 1—3 against 2—4. It is not so easy to see from the draft what combination of harnesses will weave the A block or any other block. However, the twill nature of the draft indicates correctly that the pattern tie-up is the standard twill tie-up. Since the pattern of crackle is a twill and two pattern blocks are always woven at the same time, no combination of harnesses can be said to be *the* combination that will produce any one block. Each combination of two harnesses weaves two pattern blocks. The 1—2 combination weaves Blocks A and B; 2—3 weaves Blocks B and C; 3—4 weaves Blocks C and D and the 1—4 combination weaves Blocks A and D (Fig. 182).

Treadling. Fig. 183 is a diagram analysis of crackle, and as is customary in this sort of diagram (see also Figs. 147, 148), the tabby shots are not shown. The first four weft threads are woven on the 1—2 combination of harnesses. The A block has a group of three adjacent threads on harnesses 1 and 2; the B block also has a group of three adjacent threads on harnesses 1 and 2. Therefore, when the pattern weft is woven on the 1—2 combination, both Block A and Block B have three-thread overshots to form the pattern block (Fig. 182). In the same way there is a 2—3 combination in Block B and in Block C; there is a 3—4 combination in Block C and in Block D; and there is a 1—4 combination in Block D and in

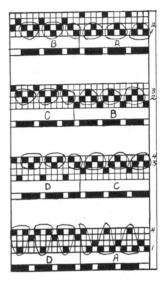

Figure 182

Block A. This explains why two pattern blocks are woven at the same time and why the draft dictates which two blocks will combine. The weaver has no choice. Both Fig. 182 and Fig. 183 show

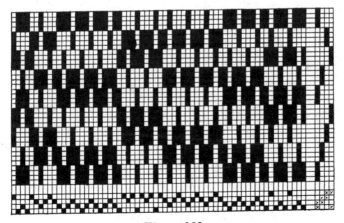

Figure 183

clearly the small two-thread overshot which apparently occurs in the middle of a woven pattern block, but which structurally occurs between the blocks.

In actual practice the weaving process is not so different from that of summer-and-winter. Every pattern shot is followed by a tabby shot, and as many pattern shots are used as may be desired or needed. Also, as in other weaves, the pattern may be varied almost endlessly by varying the order of treadling and the number of pattern shots in the various blocks. As a rule it takes two pattern shots and two tabby shots to weave one unit of the pattern draft. The choice of yarns may change the number of shots needed, but if the yarns are in balance, the four weft shots will square up with the four warp threads in each unit.

It is not always the simplest matter to find the treadling draft, given the threading draft only. For instance, if the draft at Fig. 179 is to be woven as drawn in, the treadling will be 3 units of C; 4 of B; 3 of C; 2 of A; 1 of B; 1 of A; 1 of B; 2 of A. There is no combination of harnesses which will weave only one block, so it is not possible to count on weaving the A block with the harness combination of 1—2, or the B with 2—3, and so on. If this were the way of finding the treadling, the design might very well end up looking like Fig. 184, which of course is no design at all.

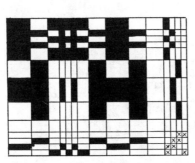

Figure 184

The most satisfactory way to find the treadling is to make a diagram of the pattern as at Fig. 171. The first section of the pattern woven is the combined Blocks B and C. Since the B block is put on the #2 harness and the C block on the #3 harness, the combination of harnesses 2 and

3 will weave this section of the pattern. The next section of the pattern is a C block alone. In crackle, no block can be woven singly because two harnesses must always be used at a time. In this design there is no D block threaded into the harnesses, so if the 3—4 harnesses are used, there being no D to weave, C will weave alone. The next section, like the first, is woven 2—3. This completes the square box-like part of the pattern. The next part of the pattern calls for the A block alone, and, like the single C block, it is woven in combination with the nonexistent D block, and is treadled 1—4.

In writing treadling directions, one must remember that there are both rising shed and falling shed looms. In actual weaving, if it is necessary to transpose the treadling, this is easily enough done.

Variations. All of the foregoing instructions are for crackle in the conventional or traditional method of design and weaving. Rarely are existing designs fitted for contemporary use, and crackle on the traditional 20/2 cotton warp is most uninteresting. However, if the design has meaning and is suitable for its intended use, and if the yarns are well chosen, crackle woven in the conventional method can be most effective. This is admirably illustrated by the dossal (Fig. 185) woven by Tina Mc-Morran for the Methodist Church in Gatlinburg, Tennessee. The diagram of a portion of the design is shown at Fig. 186.

The twill nature of a crackle draft suggests a twill treadling for a texture weave. With a quite heavy warp set close together, a simple twill (1-2-3-4) treadling gives a rough surface with no particular pattern. It does not make much difference what the threading draft is, the resulting fabrics are all more or less alike. A better fabric, because the herringbone effect of the twill is less obvious, is obtained by an irregular treadling or a broken twill treadling (Fig. 187).

Figure 185

Figure 186

The use of interesting yarns can do much for crackle. Novelty yarns in both warp and tabby will lift crackle into contemporary value. Small spots of pattern can be scattered over the surface so that the pattern is decoration only without dominating the fabric. Fig. 188 shows such a fabric; both the warp and tabby weft are alternately carpet warp and cotton bouclé; the pattern weft is a large soft-twist worsted.

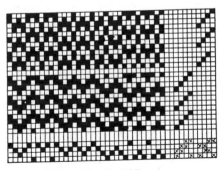

Figure 187

Figure 188

The value of novelty yarns to crackle is dramatically shown at Fig. 189. The inset shows a rather small and very simple crackle pattern woven in the conventional manner—20/2 cotton warp and tabby, the pattern weft the usual soft floss. While this design is less objectionable than many of the big and sprawling patterns, it is certainly far from making an inspired or inspiring pattern. The larger piece shown is the selfsame pattern. The yarns used are cotton bouclé for warp, a soft-twisted mercerized for pattern and a fine rayon for tabby. All three are of practically the same color value. This particular piece drapes beautifully. The same yarns in the same weave, but sleyed more closely and beaten more firmly, make an equally good upholstery fabric.

Figure 189

There are two ways of doing crackle in polychrome. One method is illustrated at Fig. 190. In each block of pattern there are two groups that make small overshots. In the A block these groups are the 1—2 and the 1—4, in the C block the groups are 3—4 and 2—3. Two colors of pattern weft are used, one on each of the two groups. A tabby must be used with this type of treadling; it is not shown in the illustration for it would make the diagram too confused. Whether the tabby follows each pattern shot or follows the pair of pattern wefts will depend on the type of yarn used and the effect desired. Either

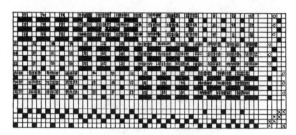

Figure 190

way is permissible. Color also will help to decide where the tabby is used. This type of treadling demands a simple pattern and is usually better on a rather coarse fabric.

The second polychrome method is a method on opposites. In crackle there are only pattern and background. If 1—2 is woven in the pattern color, then 3—4 in a background color, the whole surface of the fabric will be weft-faced. When the design calls for the pattern to be woven on 3—4, the background will be woven on 1—2. Crackle is not a good fabric to be woven entirely on opposites, for the three warps in a group tend to pull together and the fabric becomes loose and sleazy. A tabby must be used, and usually it is better to use the tabby after a pair of wefts rather than after each weft. The tabby should be fine and inconspicuous almost to the point of invisibility. This type of treadling makes good rugs. The warp should be heavy and stiff and rather widely spaced in the loom. The pattern wefts should be soft enough to pack firmly and to cover as nearly as possible the tabby wefts. The tabby must be strong enough to keep the warps in place and should match in color either the pattern or the background weft.

Fig. 191 is a diagram of a small portion of a crackle weave. The treadling draft indicates the tabby as well as the pattern weft, the pattern weft being shown as black squares and the tabby weft as small circles. In the diagram the tabby foundation

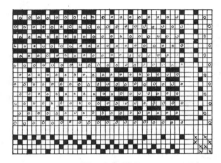

Figure 191

of the cloth is also represented by the small circles in order to avoid confusion with the black squares of the pattern wefts. It is the treadling draft that is the important part of this diagram. This draft looks like a threading draft for summer-and-winter written vertically instead of horizontally. With the fabric of Fig. 13 in Chapter 2 as precedent, the diagram was turned to make the treadling draft become the threading draft. This diagram was made in terms of a *rising* shed so that the warp overshots could be represented by the black squares. The foundation warps of this summer-and-winter draft on harnesses 1 and 2, as well as the wefts, are represented by small circles, again to avoid confusion with the pattern warps.

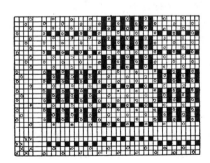

Figure 192

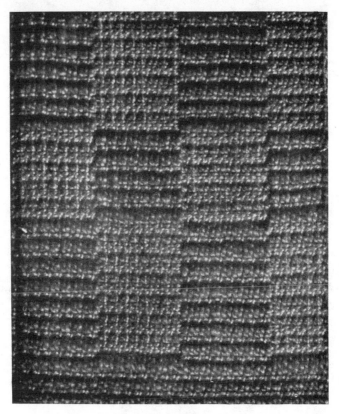

Figure 193

To prove that the theory of transposition was correct as well as practical, a sample was woven on the loom. The foundation warps on harnesses 1 and 2 and the weft were 10/2 cotton; No. 3 perle cotton was used for the pattern warps. The draft of Fig. 192 was used as a model, but larger blocks were threaded. Only the foundation warps were taken into consideration when the sley was determined. The pattern warps lie on top of the fabric and so have no effect on the foundation of the cloth. Treadling follows the order as shown in Fig. 192. Detail of the resulting fabric is shown at Fig. 193.

This adaptation of crackle has much to recommend it. The fact that in a four-harness loom there are possible only two blocks of pattern assures simple designs. As it is a one-shuttle weave, it is quick and easy to do. In proper yarns and colors it is a fabric suitable for upholstery, bags, and other objects calling for sturdy material. It is rather heavy to drape well. Warp overshots are relatively rare in handwoven fabrics and for that reason, if for no other, they can look handmade without looking homemade. New designs can be made, new variations of weave can be found, so that crackle may become a more useful weave.

PROBLEMS

1. Translate an ordinary four-block pattern to a crackle pattern. Change the proportions where necessary to make a better-looking design.
2. Choose a portion of the above design and develop that portion to make a simpler, more interesting pattern.
3. Write drafts for both of the above patterns.
4. Make a design using a broken twill in the pattern draft.
5. Write the drafts for the above.

CHAPTER 11

Colonial Overshot

"Overshot," this weave most certainly is, but how "Colonial" is open to debate. The very early colonists from England did not bring it over with them, for it is only in comparatively recent years that this type of weaving has been known and used in England. It seems to have been brought to this country by the Scandinavian colonists, and because of its usefulness and adaptability became popular and spread widely and rapidly.

In the library of the Metropolitan Museum in New York City there are a number of books and manuscripts dating back to 1704 that were published in Germany or written in German, in which the designs shown are practically identical in most cases with the traditional patterns of Colonial overshot as we know it. But in the German books the directions are for the "Double Kolsch," which is the well-known blue and white double-woven coverlet of the period before the advent of the Jacquard loom in 1826.

The weave is well suited to the counterbalanced loom— which was the type of most of the early looms. It is the easiest way to get combinations of pattern and color and it is adaptable to almost any kind of weaving material. Most early Americans grew flax and raised sheep, so linen and wool yarns were easily available. Calicoes and similar fabrics, on the other hand, had to be imported from England, and consequently "pieces" for quilts were precious. It was natural that the woven bed "kiver" should become popular—materials were at hand and it was much less work to weave a wool coverlet than to piece a quilt. It is only in the American revival of handweaving in the twentieth century that we have used this weave for all sorts of inappropriate articles from dresses and coats to curtains and up-

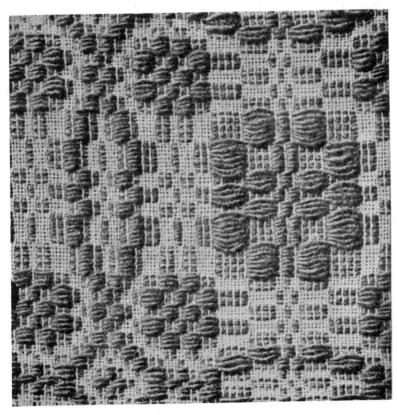

Figure 194

holstery, instead of confining it to the use for which it is well adapted.

In the Scandinavian countries the weave is sometimes called "halvdrejl" but most commonly it is called "Daldräll" or literally "twill from Dalecarlia (Dalarne)." It is widely used in those countries for a number of fabrics, but in most cases it is a much finer cloth than we in America have been weaving— 40 to 60 ends per inch make it look very different from our commonplace 30 per inch fabric.

For many years after the revival of handweaving in America, this was the only weave we had, and consequently it was used for everything and anything—usually on a 20/2 white or natural cotton warp at 30 ends per inch! It was inevitable that it should come to be sneered at and discarded by sophisticated weavers. But it is adaptable to so many variations that when it is properly used it is a most valuable weave. If only American weavers would give up white warps of 20/2 cotton at 30 ends per inch, Colonial overshot would be greatly improved!

Apparent characteristics. Perhaps the most obvious characteristic of Colonial overshot is the distinguishing characteristic —it is a *three-tone* weave. The pattern stands out boldly and clearly, being formed by overshots (or floats, or skips) of the pattern weft. There are two kinds of background weave—blocks of plain tabby weave and blocks of a tabby weave with the pattern color combined with the tabby weft (Fig. 194). No other of the general types of handwoven fabrics has this three-tone effect.

It is a three-thread construction. There is a single warp, but two wefts—a pattern weft and a tabby weft. The pattern blocks are formed by the pattern weft only. The background is formed partly by blocks of plain tabby and partly by blocks in which the pattern weft combines with the tabby weft to make the mixed or half-tone effect.

The structure of the fabric is the same on both sides, but the pattern is usually quite different. What is overshot on one side is tabby on the reverse. The half-tone sections are the same on both sides.

Usually the tabby weft is the same as the warp or slightly finer, and the pattern weft is heavier. In a well-constructed piece of Colonial overshot, if the pattern wefts could be removed from the cloth, a perfectly good piece of plain tabby cloth would remain.

Colonial overshot is usually a four-block pattern. There are many two-block patterns known as Monk's Belt; occasionally three-block patterns are found. Patterns of more than four blocks require more than a four-harness loom and are a classification to themselves.

Structural characteristics. The apparent characteristics are also structural, for as in all handwoven patterns, it is the structure that makes the pattern. The chief structural characteristic that cannot be seen in the finished cloth is the type of threading draft. Each block of pattern is formed by a group of threads on two adjacent harnesses, and these groups usually are in the form of a twill. Simply stated, the draft for Colonial overshot is a repeat twill.

At Fig. 195 is a diagram analysis of a portion of Colonial

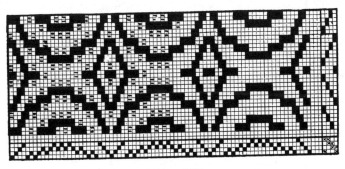

Figure 195

overshot. The object of making a diagram analysis is either (a) to find the draft, given the finished pattern; or (b) to find the pattern, given the draft, and to check for mistakes in the draft. In either case, the binder or tabby weft is of little consequence; it is the pattern weft that is important. The diagram disregards the tabby weft, for it would only confuse the picture. In making the diagram, the half-tone may or may not be taken into consideration. It is of little help in finding the draft from the woven piece, for the overshots alone are really important. In making the diagram from the draft, the half-tone is of little help in visualizing the pattern, for the woven effect is so very different from the effect on paper. In Fig. 195 the overlapping of two adjacent blocks by one warp thread is easily visible. One half of the diagram shows the half-tones, while the other half shows only the overshots.

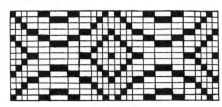

Figure 196

Fig. 196 shows the same pattern drawn in purely diagram form without regard to the actual warp threads. It is perhaps easier to work from this sort of diagram when writing a threading draft.

Draft writing. Colonial overshot is really a twill with pairs of warps on two adjacent harnesses repeated to form the overshots. The threading draft is most easily written by applying the formula for each unit to the pattern draft. Generally speaking, the A block is placed on harnesses 1 and 2; the B block is on harnesses 2 and 3; the C block is on harnesses 3 and 4; and

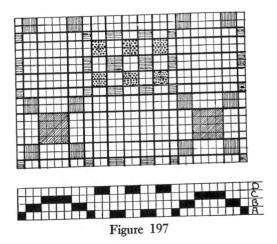

Figure 197

finally the D block is on harnesses 4 and 1. Usually the two warp threads make one unit of design. If there are three units of Block A, the draft is written 1-2-1-2-1-2.

At Fig. 197 is a pattern drawn on squared paper with the blocks filled in to represent A, B, C, D, and with heavy crosslines drawn to keep the boundaries of the various blocks. Directly below it is the pattern draft. Beginning at the lower right corner, the first block is A and contains only one unit of design; therefore the draft begins with 1—2. The next block is B and contains two units of design or four warp threads, written on the draft 2-3-2-3. Because there is one warp common to two adjacent blocks, the last thread of one block becomes the first thread of the following block and only 3-2-3 is added to the draft (Fig. 198). In the next block, C has four units or eight threads, which means that 4-3-4-3-4-3-4 is added to the draft, making a total of eight threads in the group forming the C block. But this Block C is a reversing block, the following one being another B, or 2—3, block. A 2 may not be placed next to a 4 because of the tabby combination; so in this case, the C block is 3—2. The order in which the threads appear on the

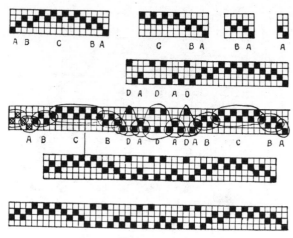

Figure 198

draft is of no consequence so far as the block is concerned. When the shed is opened, 2-3-2-3 is no different from 3-2-3-2.

In this case, 3-2-3-2 is added to the draft for the second B block. There are no longer eight threads in the C group but there are nine. It is always true of a Colonial overshot draft that so long as the blocks proceed in a single direction, there will be an even number of warps in any block; but when the direction of progression changes, there will be an odd number of warps in the group forming the reversing block.

The design at Fig. 197 calls for eight threads in the C block, but because it is a reversing block, there must be either seven or nine ends. There is no rule to tell whether a reversing block has one more or one less thread. This must be left to the discretion of the weaver. The size of the yarn and the count of the reed used for a particular piece should help to decide whether to add or subtract the extra thread.

Since the B block ended with a 2, it remains only to write a single 1 in order to complete the draft for the first group of A, B, C, B, A.

The sixth block of the pattern is a two-unit, four-thread D block, using the combination of 1-4-1-4. But this D block is a reversing block, as are all three D blocks in the pattern. The two A blocks between the D blocks are also reversing blocks. All five of these blocks will call for odd numbers of warp-ends. If variety is desired in this center group of D, A, D, A, D, the center D might be given five threads and the others three threads each. For the sake of illustration this was done in one of the drafts at Fig. 198, but of course this changed the proportions of the design as originally made.

To keep the proportions as nearly as possible to the original design, one should be consistent and always add or always subtract the extra warp-end. If sometimes a thread is added and sometimes dropped, the design can soon lose balance. And after any draft is written, it should be checked to see that both sides are alike *if* they are intended to be alike. A design need not be bisymmetrical, but if it is meant to balance evenly a difference of even two-warp threads looks most obviously like the mistake it is. If the blocks are not meant to be the same size, see that there is enough difference in the number of warp-ends in the blocks so that they really *look* different.

The third group of blocks in the pattern of Fig. 197 is identical with the first group and can be written exactly as was the first part of the draft. When considering the second repeat of the pattern, one finds that the final A block of the pattern is also the first A block of the second repeat and that the A block is a reversing block and will have three threads in it. For practical purposes, an overshot of nine is likely to be too long. Although the result is a change in the proportions of the original design, in the finished draft at the bottom of Fig. 198 the C blocks have been made smaller, while the A and D blocks are all the same size.

It is perfectly possible to write the draft for any design

in a number of ways. Especially is this true when one is writing a draft from a finished piece of weaving. The beginning of the repeat may be at any one of the various blocks in that repeat. Obviously, then, there may be as many different drafts as there are blocks in any horizontal row of the pattern.

With a given design (for example the design at Fig. 197) and with the stipulation that the draft must begin at a given block, there are still at least twelve different drafts possible. If 1—3 and 2—4 are reserved for the tabby sheds, Block A may be placed on any one of the four remaining pairs of harnesses, 1—2 or 2—3 or 3—4 or 4—1. If 1—2 and 3—4 are reserved for tabby, Block A may be on 1—3, 2—3, 1—4 or 2—4. And similarly, by reserving 1—4 and 2—3 for tabby, Block A may be 1—2, 1—3, 3—4, or 2—4.

There is no very practical purpose served by writing any one draft in so many different ways, or even in more than one way. But a draft can hold no possible terror for any weaver who has it so thoroughly under control that he can write it in any form. The first half of the corrected draft at Fig. 198 is shown in various disguises at Fig. 199. See also Fig. 8 in Chapter 2.

Colonial overshot may also be drafted on opposites. The most familiar type of this sort of draft is the two-block Monk's Belt. With only two blocks in the pattern and these two blocks placed on opposite pairs of harnesses, there are in the woven

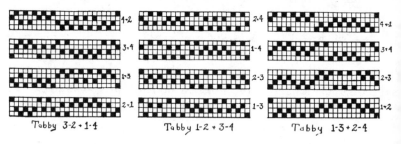

Figure 199

Figure 200

cloth only overshot pattern blocks and tabby backgrounds. There is no half-tone. (For illustration of Monk's Belt, see Fig. 215 in Chapter 12.)

Four-block patterns can also be drafted on opposites. If the A block is placed on the 1—2 pair of harnesses, the next block, the B block, is placed on the opposite pair of harnesses— the 3—4 combination. The C block is placed on the 2—3 pair of harnesses and the opposite or 1—4 combination on the D block as usual.

Drafting on opposites changes the position of the two kinds of background. In patterns woven on the regular drafts, or those drafted to twill, there is always a half-tone block between the overshot pattern block and the tabby background block. When the pattern is drafted on opposites the tabby will be immediately next to the pattern and the half-tones for the other two blocks will be combined in one area. Compare Fig. 200 with Fig. 201. Both are simple diamond patterns, but Fig. 200 is drafted to twill while Fig. 201 is drafted on opposites.

The draft for Fig. 201 is given at Fig. 202. There are a number of items to note in this draft. In the first place, the A and D blocks are reversing blocks, and as in the twilled draft there are an uneven number of warp-ends in reversing blocks. The A block is on 1—2 and the B block on 3—4.

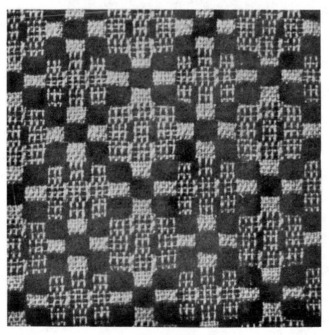

Figure 201

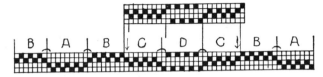

Figure 202

Where these two blocks join, there is a 2—3 combination of only two warp-ends. When the cloth is woven, this single 2—3 combination is ignored; but when the C block, also on 2—3 is woven, the little two-warp overshot will appear automatically. These are accidentals that cannot be avoided unless a 4 is placed next to a 2, and that would spoil the tabby, a result which would be worse.

B is not a reversing block, but because of the 2—3 that follows it, there must of necessity be an odd number of ends in the B block. Between every two blocks there is either a little two-warp overshot or a single warp-end that is common to the two adjacent blocks. In the treadling these small two-warp overshots are not woven, but in the draft they must be controlled. Note in the draft that on each side of the D or 1—4 block, the accidentals are 1—2. Then note that above the draft a short section has been written. On one side of the D block, the accidental is 3—4 and on the other side it is 1—2. Note in Fig. 201 that these little overshots are quite obvious. If they are consistently in the same relative position they are much less distracting than if scattered around in a seemingly haphazard fashion.

There is little advantage in writing a draft on opposites— Colonial overshot as a type of weave is no longer fashionable. Its chief value is in weaving honeycomb, but uses for honeycomb, especially on four blocks, are definitely limited. It can be useful sometimes in writing a special draft for a lace or textured effect.

Tie-up. There is little to be said about tie-up. Colonial over-shot, being a twill weave, automatically calls for the standard tie-up. In most drafts, 1—3 weaves one tabby and 2—4 weaves the other. And usually 1—2 weaves the A block, 2—3 weaves the B block, 3—4 weaves the C block, and 1—4 weaves the D block.

The type of loom has something to do with what harnesses weave what block. For the drafts at Fig. 198, if the loom has a falling shed, pulling down harnesses 1 and 2 will put the A block on the visible side of the fabric while it is being woven. If harnesses 1 and 2 are pulled *up*, the A block will weave on the under side of the fabric as it is on the loom.

Treadling. Since this is a three-thread construction, it is axiomatic that a tabby weft must follow every pattern weft. With Colonial overshot, more than with most weaves, it is difficult to make hard and fast rules for treadling. Theoretically, it takes one pattern shot and one tabby shot to weave a single unit of a block. If there are two warp-ends in a pattern block, one pattern weft and one tabby weft should weave that block; if there are four warp-ends, supposedly two pattern and two tabby wefts should weave the block. But this will not always work; much depends on the balance in size of the yarns and in the number of ends per inch. If the pattern is to be woven as drawn in and in the conventional manner, it is better to follow the pattern blocks on the diagonal and to use as many pattern wefts as are needed to make the block square. Usually the fabric is better looking if the balance between the warp and the two wefts is such that it takes two shots of pattern and two of tabby to weave a single unit of pattern.

Most important in determining the number of shots to put in each block is the relation of the tabby to the pattern. In large patterns an extra shot more or less will not show, but in small patterns one shot may make a tremendous difference. It is

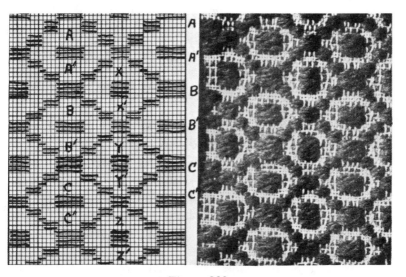

Figure 203

not possible to make a simple rule that says: always use this or that tabby first. It just won't work. The nearest thing to a simple rule is: always use an even number of pattern shots, particularly at a block where the treadling reverses direction.

This is illustrated at Fig. 203. On one side is a photograph of an area of a small all-over pattern. Beside it is a diagram of the same area; to avoid confusion the half-tones and the tabby are not shown. In the photograph the background area of A looks quite different from the area of A'; but A' looks like B, and again, B is different from B'. On the diagram can be seen the *reason* for the differences. There are on *odd* number of shots in the reversing block between A and A', and between B and B', and between C and C'. Between A' and B and between B' and C there are an *even* number of shots in the reversing blocks. In the XYZ column we find similar differences. In the ABC column the two halves of each little motif do not seem to belong to each other, while in the XYZ column there seem to be two different small patterns that alternate. In the diagram can be seen some very small overshots which hardly show in the photograph. There is only one at a time—an odd number—but because there is one in each half of the pattern, they balance each other, and two odd numbers added together give an even number.

In the A area a mistake in treadling was made—the small shot was left out, and extra shots were put in the other two groups. There are six shots in the A area, but five in all other similar areas. These single shots are not at reversing points, which is one reason that they have no effect on the pattern.

There may be a rule somewhere that will tell us what to do to start the tabby in the right relation to the pattern, but if there is such a rule it is sure to be most complicated. It is far easier to weave a few shots for an inch or two to see if the effect obtained is the proper one; if it is not, then try the opposite tabby. When the weaving is started properly, keep it that way by reversing with an *even* number of shots in the block. The question naturally arises: which of the two sides of the motif is the correct one? The answer is simple: whichever the weaver prefers.

The proper relation of tabby to pattern weft may seem a small problem, but it is the small detail that often makes the difference between a weave that looks right and one that worries us because there is something about it that is not just right, although we can't find what it is. A glaring error is not so annoying.

A diagram of a small draft is given at Fig. 204. It is woven as drawn in and the tabby is indicated.

Colonial overshot in its traditional form is essentially a bedspread weave. On a four-poster bed in a Cape Cod house, a blue and white coverlet really "belongs." Colonial overshot can still be a good coverlet weave in twentieth century houses *if*

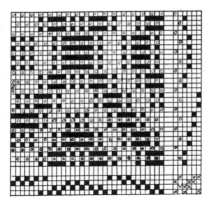

Figure 204

we discard the blue and white tradition. An all-white one is handsome. Colored ones can be good too if warp and weft are one color. But it is in the variations of the *weave* that Colonial overshot is most valuable in modern weaving. Just rearranging the blocks may change the *pattern*—for better or for worse— but it does not kill the bedspread look. Fortunately, there are many more valuable variations possible.

Variations. Almost any Colonial overshot draft, if the skips are not too long, will produce a texture weave. Use a fine warp set very close in the reed. Even the uninteresting 20/2 cotton, if sleyed at 50 or 60 per inch, can be treadled in a twill to produce a good and attractive fabric. This sort of fabric is usually more interesting in fine yarns than in heavy ones.

There are several treadlings that can be used successfully on one or another drafts. The straight twill treadling of 1—2, 2—3, 3—4, 4—1 is usually less interesting than the broken twill of 1—2, 2—3, 1—4, 3—4. Another interesting treadling on almost any draft, whether it be a straight twill of 1-2-3-4 or a complicated pattern draft is 1—3, 2—3, 2—4, 1—4. The secret of the texture weaves is that they must be sleyed closely.

The draft at A of Fig. 205 would not make a particularly

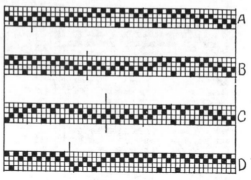

Figure 205

interesting fabric if woven in a twill for a textured effect—all groups are nearly the same size, and seven ends in a group would make a rather long overshot, even at a close sley. Reduce it in size and have some variation in the number of ends in a group and the fabric will be greatly improved (B of Fig. 205).

Reduce the draft still further and use it as a dummy. This weave need not be so closely sleyed, for it will use four different yarns in the warp. Tie one type of yarn to the ends on the #1 harness, tie the second yarn to the ends on the #2 harness, the third yarn on harness 3, and finally the fourth yarn to the warp-ends on the #4 harness. A more interesting arrangement of the yarns will result than if the four yarns are wound on the warp at one time and arranged in a 1, 2, 3, 4 sequence. Four colors may be substituted for four kinds of yarn, or a combination of color and variation of size or texture in the yarn can be used. This gives a very definite stripe effect, so colors must be chosen carefully.

Open lace stripes can very well be woven on Colonial overshot. D of Fig. 205 is essentially the same draft. Two of the C blocks have been greatly enlarged—too much to be used in treadling. If alternate shots of weft are combinations that contain either harness 3 or harness 4, then the area of the C block will weave in a tabby. With the 1—2 and the 3—4 combinations of treadles eliminated because the overshots would be much too long, there are left 1—3, 2—4, 2—3 and 1—4. In that order, 3 and 4 alternate, but 1 and 2 weave in pairs. Another treadling is shown in the diagram at Fig. 206. Depending on the yarn used and the sley, this fabric may be either an open lace or a closed texture. Illustrations of these fabrics are in Chapter 12.

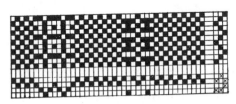

Figure 206

Bound weaving in which the wefts entirely cover the warp is very successful on Colonial overshot drafts. It makes a splendid type of fabric for upholstery or bags: it is smooth surfaced, firm, and durable. Its one disadvantage is that it weaves so slowly—about half an hour per inch is a fair average rate. The wefts are closely packed—sometimes as many as 100 per inch. There are several types of bound weaving, but certain rules must be followed in all types.

The most important single item is the balance between warp and weft. The warp must be sturdy and sleyed far enough apart so that the wefts will pack and completely cover it. On the other hand, they must not be so far apart that the wefts will pack unnecessarily close. The weft must be soft and fine. Ordinary carpet warp at 15 or 16 per inch or 40/2 linen at 20 or 24 per inch work well with 18/2 worsted if it is not a hard-twisted yarn. The three-strand Persian rug yarn will cover carpet warp if the warp is sleyed at 5 per inch. Only a very small pattern could be used in this case. The yarn is not a soft fiber to begin with and is not a soft twist in the second place. In most cases, the finer yarns for weft are much more satisfactory. Always, in any type of bound weaving, the weft must be well beaten up—the warp must not show.

If the warp is sleyed far enough apart, Colonial overshot can be treadled in the standard way—a tabby following every pattern weft. The half-tones will be subordinated to a certain extent and the whole background will have a tapestry effect. Naturally much depends on the pattern, but it is generally a good weave for rugs. Use a stiff warp, and probably Persian rug yarn for pattern and cotton chenille for tabby. The chenille has enough texture to hide the warp and half-tone, and it will pack very closely. The rug will have body and if a simple diamond pattern is used, it will never suggest a bedspread.

Another form of bound weaving is woven on opposites. The pattern is kept in this form of weaving, but it does not have much of the appearance of Colonial overshot in its traditional form. Usually it looks better with two tones of one color, different enough to show up but not to contrast sharply. The pattern is treadled as desired, but instead of a tabby following each pattern shot, the opposite pair of harnesses is used. If the pattern block to be woven is 1—2, then the opposite pair, or 3—4, is the binder. When 2—3 is pattern, 1—4 is binder; when 3—4 is pattern, 1—2 is binder. The wefts should pack down to cover the warps. The pattern will stand out in one color and what would be the tabby will have overshots of the binder color. The half-tone areas will be small two-tone stripes. This type of weave has a good surface interest and is very sturdy. The texture is the same on both sides; the pattern is the same but with colors reversed. The pattern should not be a complicated one. A detail is shown at Fig. 207.

Bound weaving in stripes loses all semblance to pattern or to the structure of Colonial overshot. Four colors are used,

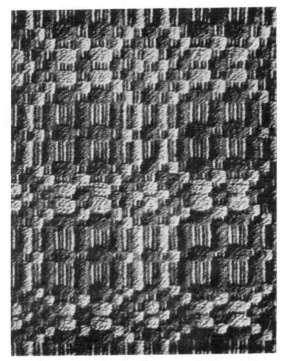

Figure 207

all of the same kind of yarn. The treadling is a simple twill and it never varies. Each color is always woven on the same combination: color A on 1—2, color B on 2—3, color C on 3—4 and color D on 1—4. The draft is important in this weave, not because of the pattern as such, but because of proportion. The draft at A of Fig. 205 is a poor one for this type of weave on two counts. First, the pattern blocks or groups of warp-ends are all nearly the same size; and second, the grouping of B, A, B, A, B makes a grouping of two colors alternating with an equal grouping of two other colors on Blocks C, D, C, D, C. There would be two wide stripes each divided into two narrow stripes, and all stripes the same size. Color is important also—the brightest colors will need to be on the smallest overshots, and colors that are near in value will lose identity when next to each other. It is only by experimenting on the loom that the proper relationship of the colors to each other can be determined.

Flame Point is another form of bound weaving and is a natural outgrowth of the striped weaving. In texture and structure they are the same. Color makes the pattern of both, but Flame Point has more pattern. The stripes may be of contrasting colors, but Flame Point demands four shades of one color or four closely related colors. Yellow shading to green, or yellow shading to brown will work, but a mixture of blues and reds loses the continuity of the pattern.

Flame Point is woven with four shuttles on a direct twill treadling, but the colors shift at stated intervals to make the pattern. Treadle 1—2 with shade A; treadle 2—3 with shade B; treadle 3—4 with shade C and finally treadle 1—4 with shade D. These four shots are repeated the proper number of times and then the colors are shifted. Treadle 1—2 with shade B; 2—3 with shade C, 3—4 with D and 1—4 with A. The order of treadling never changes. After the desired number of shots in this sequence, the shuttles are shifted again so that 1—2 is woven with C; 2—3 with D, and so on till all four combinations have been used and repeated. The shuttles are shifted for the fourth time so that 1—2 is woven with shade D, and the A, B, and C shades follow in their correct sequence. The treadling never changes from the direct twill order of 1—2, 2—3, 3—4, 1—4. It takes one shot of each color, each over its proper group of warp-ends, to make one complete line of color across the cloth. Each group of four shots is repeated to make the amount desired of one color before the colors are shifted.

In weaving this fabric, one should remember the proverb: make haste slowly. An attempt to hurry will result in tangled wefts, mixed colors, and lost time in picking up the wrong shuttle. If after each shot the shuttle is laid in its proper order, one following the other, on the finished web (not woven too close to the breast beam) the rhythm and economy of motion will make for more speed. Even so, it is a slow weave.

The angle of the points may be more or less acute, according to the treadling. If only four shots of each color are used before shifting, naturally the angle will be flatter than if there are ten or more shots in a group. This is illustrated in the diagram at Fig. 208. The design is more interesting if the number of warps in a group is varied. The number of wefts may or may not vary. A of Fig. 209 is most uninteresting; B is a bit better. C would be improved by having more wefts in each group so that the "flame" is more pointed.

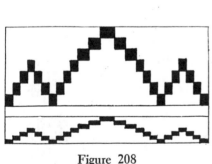

Figure 208

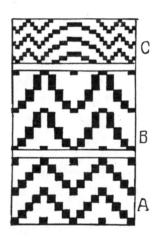

Figure 209

Designs are made for Flame Point by planning the dominating line—what the draft looks like as a pattern is unimportant. Patterns should not be large as a rule. If the warp is to be sleyed at 20 or 24 per inch, a draft of 40 or 50 ends will make a "flame" two inches wide. This might be rather large for some uses.

Honeycomb is a variation in weave on a Colonial overshot draft that has little resemblance to the traditional form of the weave. It may be interpreted in a wide variety of ways. In Sweden it is often done in very fine yarns—as many as 80 per inch in the warp. It is done in all white and is often used for men's shirts because, as one weaver from Dalarne explained, "it wears so unending." It may be done in a very "free" interpretation such as the one shown in Chapter 12. It is a weave for which there seems to be no very attractive middle ground. It has a three-dimensional look, but its uses are limited because of the long skips on the reverse side. It is not a good upholstery material because when it is stretched, it loses the depth which is its chief charm. Two-block patterns do not have the long skips on the under side, and in the two-block version the weave is quite often used for bedspreads. It is partly woven by treadling one harness at a time and consequently is not too easily done on a counterbalanced loom.

Two weft yarns are used, one equal, or nearly equal, in size to the warp yarn and the other much heavier—three to six times the size of the main weft. The blocks are woven individually with fine weft, making small blocks of plain weaving, and after each block is so woven,

Figure 210

there are two shots of tabby with the heavy yarn. The heavy weft shots make the "walls" and the fine wefts make the "cells" of the honeycomb. This is the more or less standard way of weaving honeycomb, but it too has variations.

Fig. 210 shows a portion of a draft with the standard treadling. Note in the treadling draft that the fine wefts are so woven that they do not come in the same shed at any place with the heavy tabby. At the beginning of the treadling draft, the second heavy tabby is on the 2—4 combination; the first fine tabby is not on the #2 but on the #1 harness.

Figure 211

An interesting variation on the honeycomb theme is obtained by the method indicated at Fig. 211. The two blocks in two different sizes are arranged to make interesting groupings of stripes. One weft is used and it is the same size as the warp. The treadling may follow either of the two methods shown or they may be alternated.

Pattern blocks for honeycomb must not be too large because of the overshots on the reverse side. On the other hand, blocks of only two or three warp-ends are likely to lose their identity and become lost.

Figure 212

A variation of Colonial overshot which is reminiscent of Flame Point, but in which the character of the weave is not so completely lost, is achieved by the use of three weft yarns. The

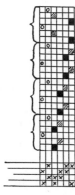

sample shown at Fig. 212 shows the structure of the weave. The method of treadling is shown at Fig. 213. Each group of wefts is repeated as many times as desired. As in Flame Point, the more often each group is repeated, the more slender the "flame" grows.

Figure 213

In this weave the tabby portion of the background is eliminated. Woven in soft yarns and with a light beat, the fabric makes a good drapery; woven in harder yarns and with a heavy beat, it makes a satisfactory upholstery. In any case the pattern should be chosen with care to make an interesting outline. There should not be much contrast in color; interest should depend on texture. The sample shown in Chapter 12 is a more interesting fabric than the sample here.

Because of its variations rather than its traditional form, Colonial overshot is worth knowing, although all variations are not equally good. Some will turn out well almost in spite of what we do with them, and others take much thought and very careful handling to make them worth while.

PROBLEMS

1. Make a design for a Colonial overshot pattern using four blocks. Write the draft for it on opposites and to twill.
2. Weave samples on both drafts in the traditional manner and in as many variations as possible.
3. Adjust the drafts as needed to improve the samples and weave them again in suitable yarns to make the fabrics really worth while.
4. Try to capitalize on a mistake made to "invent" a new method of using a Colonial overshot draft.

■.■.■.■.■.■.■.■.■.

■.■.■.■.■.■.■.■.■.

■.■.■.■.■.■.■.■.■.

CHAPTER 12

Two Themes
With Variations

The various kinds of weaves that are most commonly used by handweavers have been studied—each in its own little niche. How are they alike and how are they different? The characteristics of each have been tabulated in the chart on page 210. In this table the fabrics are considered only in their standard or conventional form; the variations of the different weaves are not considered.

In the first place, we find that the pattern in all fabrics is made in the same general way—there are overshots (or skips, or floats) in blocks of varying sizes. Though the structure may not be the same on both sides, all fabrics are reversible in that either side may be used. Of the six types of fabrics listed here, three are of two-thread construction and three are of three-thread construction. Except in summer-and-winter and in crackle, the overshots may or may not vary in size. Each weave has a distinguishing characteristic—one thing that no other weave has and which keeps it from being confused with any other weave.

It is interesting to note that three of the weaves are actually twill weaves with twill-type drafts, but with enough individuality to warrant giving them a classification of their own. M's and O's and Colonial overshot are both definite twills and even repeat twills; the only point in which they seem to differ is that one is a two-thread construction and the other a three-thread construction. The tabby background is only a partially shared characteristic. It is hard to imagine two fabrics more different in appearance, and yet both are actually twill weaves.

The next step in comparing the weaves is to take a single pattern and weave that pattern in as many different structures as possible. Two patterns have been selected.

It is hard to think of a better two-block pattern than Monk's Belt. Through the centuries it seems to have been evolving until, in its most familiar form, it has thoroughly pleasing proportions. It has developed as a Colonial overshot on opposites, but there is no reason why it should stay in that class only.

Fig. 214 shows a chart of the drafts for the various weaves done in Monk's Belt pattern. There are various sizes of squares in the drafts, each square as usual representing one warp thread.

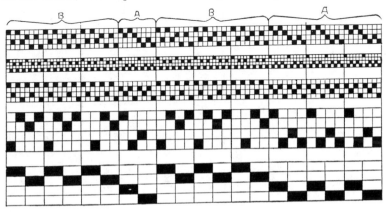

Figure 214

KIND OF WEAVE	Pattern made by overshots	Blocks may vary in size	Number of blocks possible on four harnesses	Tabby background	Structure same on both sides	Fabric reversible	Two-thread construction	Three-thread construction	Overshots standard size	Small overshots to make large blocks	Overshots parallel	Twill-type draft	DISTINGUISHING CHARACTERISTIC
M's and O's	X	X	2 (3)	X	X	X	X				X	X	Pattern and structure identical on both sides
Spot Bronson	X	X	3	X		X	X				X		Warp overshots on one side; weft overshots on reverse
Lace Bronson	X	X	2	X		X	X			X	X		Open lace-like weave. Warp and weft overshots as in Spot
Summer-and-Winter	X	X	2		X	X		X	X	X			Overshots not parallel, but staggered like bricks in a wall
Crackle	X	X	4		X	X		X	X	X	X	X	Pattern blocks combined in a twill manner
Colonial Overshot	X	X	4		X	X		X			X	X	Three-tone weave—pattern and two backgrounds

210

For lack of space, only part of the draft can be shown, but it is enough to indicate that there are three units of Block A, three of B, one of A and three of B. This is just a little more than half of the whole pattern. The chart also shows that it takes eight ends of warp to make one block of pattern in M's and O's; there are twelve ends in lace bronson; eight in summer-and-winter; four in crackle, and two in Colonial overshot.

Usually six ends is considered to be one unit of lace bronson, but it takes a minimum of two units to make one open "window"; so in order to keep the proper proportion the whole pattern has been doubled. Summer-and-winter has also been doubled—a single block can easily be lost, especially if the pattern is woven to twill, or if woven in pairs.

In the two-block crackle draft, note that there are no accidentals added; in the transition from one block to the next, one warp-end has had to be dropped.

In the Colonial overshot draft, the squares would have been too over-poweringly large if they had been drawn full size; so they were just cut in half—each rectangle represents one warp thread.

Also because of its unwieldly size, if the proportions are to be kept, the *pattern* draft has not been drawn; the blocks are indicated by the letters A and B.

Fig. 215 shows samples of the fabrics as actually woven. The pattern is the same in all of them; it is only the structure that changes. At A is the M's and O's version of Monk's Belt; at B is lace bronson; at C is summer-and-winter, and at D is the familiar Colonial overshot as we have known it for so long. There is little point in weaving any two-block pattern in crackle. Summer-and-winter is a much more interesting fabric, and if for some reason there is objection to the staggered overshots, only one of the pattern combinations for each block need be woven and the fabric will look exactly like crackle.

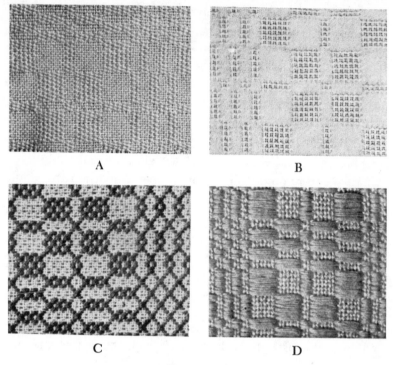

Figure 215

To weave the Monk's Belt pattern in spot bronson would hardly be practical. The difference in size of the blocks would not add to the attractiveness of the fabric, but would only make it sleazy and useless. A two-block pattern in spot bronson is really huck weave and is most interesting in its standard form.

These four weaves are shown only in their traditional forms. The variations have been left to the second pattern, for there we are not limited to four harnesses—although four harnesses have been used in most of the samples.

For the second pattern, the huck *threading* was used as a *pattern* draft and threading drafts for the various structures were developed from it. It would take a lifetime to exhaust all the possibilities of the five types of fabric done on this basic pattern, and it would take volumes to show all the variations possible.

Fig. 216 shows some of the patterns developed from the huck draft; each block is composed of two units in these four patterns. The size of the blocks may be varied, but too much variation becomes fussy. Fig. 217 is a chart of the various drafts used. The pattern draft is not drawn in for it would be much too large on this scale; instead, the pattern blocks are indicated by the letters A, B, C, D.

Figure 216

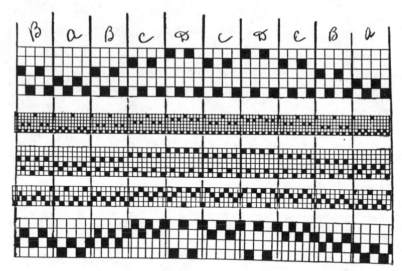

Figure 217

At Fig. 218 are the five basic weaves done on the same four-block pattern. Spot bronson is woven on five harnesses; lace bronson and summer-and-winter each require six harnesses (for the four blocks); crackle and Colonial overshot, of course, are done on four harnesses. A is spot bronson; B is lace bronson; C is summer-and-winter woven as drawn in and in single blocks to show the pattern, while D is the same pattern but with the blocks combined; E is crackle and F is Colonial overshot.

Fig. 222 is a piece of bound weaving done on the standard huck threading—not one of the pattern threadings. This is the type of bound weaving in which one harness at a time is lowered in the unbroken sequence of 1-2-3-4 and one colored weft covers each warp in turn. The treadling draft was used as the threading draft to produce the band at the left. The loom was threaded 1-2-3-4 with the colors on the proper harnesses, and then the huck threading draft was used as the treadling draft. This trick of transposing threading draft and treadling draft can be most

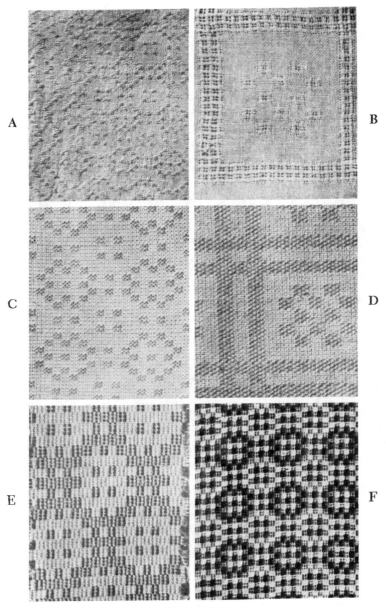

Figure 218

A   B

C   D

Figure 219.   Upper left is treadled according to Fig. 213. Upper right is flame point on the same draft. Lower left is polychrome summer-and-winter. Lower right is an experimental sample trying various yarns, each placed on a harness of its own.

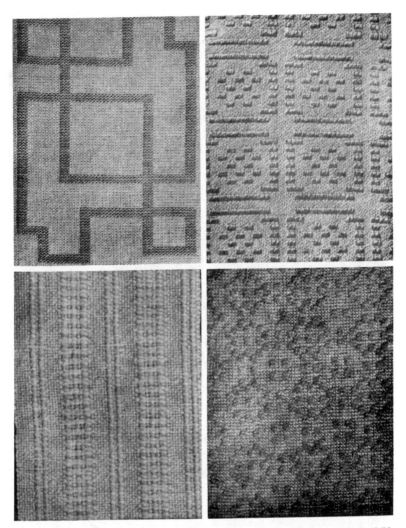

Figure 220. A picked-up summer-and-winter as described on page 153. Summer-and-winter with the pattern yarns on the pattern harnesses and woven with a single shuttle. Lower left is a Colonial overshot woven according to diagram at Fig. 206. The lower right is a spot bronson woven with both tabbies to give a very firm fabric suitable for upholstery.

A

B

Mavis Blackburn

C

Figure 221. A and B are the same draft as the Colonial overshot sample of Fig. 220; color added to the weft in the upper sample and color as well as yarn size in the lower sample make the difference. C is a honey-comb weave on the regulation Colonial overshot draft. D shows two arrangements of the draft given in the upper right of Fig. 220.

D

Figure 222

useful, not only for narrow bands, but for any kind of fabric (see also Chapter 2, Figs. 13 and 14).

Some other variations on the huck pattern theme are shown in Figs. 219, 220 and 221. In some of them the pattern is discernible and in others it is not so easy to see. In some the kind of weave is perfectly obvious, and others take a bit of study before they can be placed in their proper class of structure.

In few instances do we find that the six basic pattern weaves in their traditional forms are suitable to the demands of twentieth century styles of dress or decoration. But they are the foundation on which much can be built. There is no substitute for a thorough knowledge of the basic structures of fabrics we wish to weave. Nor can it all be learned from books or teachers. Experiment and experience are still the best roads to weaving knowledge.

Index